The Salesperson's Self-Coaching Guide

Master Your Own Self-Coaching Plan for Success

Gerard Assey

The Salesperson's Self-Coaching Guide:
Master Your Own Self-Coaching Plan for Success

By
Gerard Assey

Published by:
Gerard Assey
19/18, Palli Arasan Street
Anna Nagar East
Chennai - 600 102

ISBN: 978-81-979654-8-7

(Image courtesy Freepik: www.Freepik.com-ThankYou)

Table of Contents

Preface

Sales is a dynamic and often unpredictable profession. It's a role that requires resilience, adaptability, and a relentless drive to succeed. As someone who has walked the path of a sales professional, I know firsthand how challenging it can be to keep all the pieces moving—prospecting, building relationships, closing deals, handling objections, and, of course, maintaining a positive attitude through it all. What I've learned over the years is that success in sales doesn't just happen by chance—it happens by design.

That design comes in the form of discipline, structure, and, most importantly, self-coaching. While some salespeople are fortunate enough to have a dedicated mentor guiding them every step of the way, many of us find ourselves navigating this journey solo. This realization is what inspired me to write this book. I wanted to create a systematic, hands-on guide that any salesperson—regardless of their level of experience—could use to develop and hone their skills independently.

In sales, it's easy to feel like you're on your own. Targets loom large, pressure builds, and the path to improvement can feel unclear. This book is your blueprint for success, acting as your personal coach, with every chapter designed to address a specific aspect of the sales process. Through structured exercises, practical examples, and proven techniques, you will have a roadmap to guide your development.

The book doesn't just aim to teach you about selling—it's designed to help you create your own self-coaching plan. It will provide you with the tools you need to build discipline, track progress, and improve day by day, even without external guidance. In each chapter, you will find step-by-step instructions, worksheets, templates, and real-world scenarios, all aimed at helping you apply the lessons in a way that makes sense for your unique sales environment.

While the content covers everything from prospecting and objection handling to negotiation and customer retention, the heart of this book lies in empowering you to take control of your own growth. It's not about relying on someone else to tell you what to do next—it's about equipping you with the skills and confidence to make those decisions yourself.

In a world where many sales professionals feel under-supported and overwhelmed, this book serves as your personal toolkit, offering structure, strategy, and ongoing development. Whether you're just starting out in sales or have years of experience under your belt, you'll find that this guide offers practical, actionable insights that you can implement immediately.

Ultimately, sales is both an art and a science. It requires creativity, adaptability, and a keen understanding of human behavior, but it also requires systems, structure, and self-discipline. My hope is that, through this book, you will develop a deeper understanding of both aspects—and use that understanding to achieve long-term success.

Thank you for allowing this book to be part of your journey. It's time to take your sales career into your own hands. Let's get started.

How to Use This Book

This chapter will explain the purpose of the book, guide you on how to maximize its use, and highlight the key benefits you will gain from integrating the lessons and exercises into your daily sales routine.

Welcome to Your Personal Sales Coach

This book is designed to be more than just a guide—it's your personal coach, offering you a structured path for self-development. Sales is a fast-paced, often overwhelming profession, and not every salesperson has the privilege of a dedicated mentor or manager to guide them through challenges and opportunities. This book fills that gap, serving as your go-to resource for honing your skills, improving your performance, and creating your own self-coaching plan for success.

The tools, techniques, and exercises within this book are designed for daily use, helping you stay organized, proactive, and motivated, even when external guidance is not available. Consider it your daily playbook—a systemized approach to mastering the art and science of selling.

What You'll Learn

Through each chapter, you'll build a self-coaching system that will enable you to:

- ✓ Enhance your sales skills: From mastering the fundamentals of selling to advanced negotiation techniques, this book covers everything you need to become a more effective and successful salesperson.
- ✓ Create structure and organization: Salespeople often juggle many tasks—

prospecting, client meetings, closing deals, and follow-ups. This book helps you develop a consistent routine and stay organized so you can prioritize your tasks efficiently.

- ✓ Build self-confidence: Many sales professionals struggle with self-doubt, especially in the face of rejection or tough objections. Through guided exercises, we'll help you develop the mental resilience and confidence to overcome obstacles and thrive under pressure.
- ✓ Develop a results-oriented mindset: Whether you're new to sales or a seasoned professional, this book will shift your focus to becoming more strategic in your approach, empowering you to target the right prospects, ask the right questions, and close more deals.
- ✓ Personalize your journey: Every salesperson is different, with unique challenges, strengths, and weaknesses. The exercises and worksheets allow you to customize your plan, ensuring the strategies are relevant to your specific needs.

How to Use This Book

To get the most out of this book, we recommend actively engaging with it as you would with a real-life mentor. This is not just a book to read passively. It's a hands-on, action-based tool designed to be used daily. Here's how you can navigate and make the best use of each chapter:

- ✓ Read the chapters in sequence: Each chapter builds on the previous one, providing a step-by-step approach to improving your sales process. Start from the fundamentals and work your way through to advanced techniques.

- ✓ Complete the exercises: Each chapter includes practical worksheets, exercises, and templates that are designed to help you implement the concepts you've just learned. Don't skip them—these exercises will make the difference between understanding a concept and actually applying it in the real world. By completing them, you'll take action immediately and make measurable progress.
- ✓ Use the book as a daily reference: This book is not meant to be read once and set aside. Use it as a daily reference guide—review the chapters that are most relevant to your current challenges, revisit the templates, and keep refining your approach. Consistency is key—the more you engage with the content, the more it will become a part of your daily sales routine.
- ✓ Track your progress: Many of the exercises in this book will help you track your sales performance, identify patterns, and reflect on your successes and areas for improvement. Make it a habit to review your progress regularly so you can adjust your strategies where needed.
- ✓ Adapt the content to your situation: The book provides a wide range of strategies, templates, and examples, but it's important to tailor the material to your own unique sales environment. Whether you're selling a product or a service, in a B2B or B2C context, adjust the techniques and language to suit your industry and your customer base.

Why This Book Will Help You Succeed

Sales is one of the most dynamic and challenging professions out there. What worked yesterday might not work tomorrow, and being able to adapt, grow, and continue improving is critical to long-term success. This book will give you:

- ✓ A structured, self-paced learning system: Unlike training sessions that happen once and are forgotten, this book allows you to continually improve at your own pace, making adjustments as you learn.
- ✓ A comprehensive toolkit: From negotiation skills to handling objections and building stronger customer relationships, this book equips you with the tools you need to handle the full sales cycle—from prospecting to closing and beyond.
- ✓ Confidence in your ability to coach yourself: The exercises in this book teach you how to reflect on your performance and self-correct, a skill that will serve you well throughout your career. You'll learn how to develop strategies that are uniquely yours, instead of relying on external coaching that may not always be available.
- ✓ Proven techniques and templates: You'll have access to tried-and-tested sales techniques, along with ready-to-use templates that will save you time and effort. These are practical tools you can start using right away.
- ✓ A resource for lifelong learning: As you grow in your career, this book will grow with you. Return to it whenever you're facing a new challenge or want to refine a specific skill. The

strategies here are designed to be adaptable to various stages of your sales career.

Your Path to Sales Mastery Starts Here

If you follow the guidance in this book, complete the exercises, and commit to constant improvement, you will develop the skills, mindset, and habits needed to become a top sales professional. Success in sales requires not just knowledge, but consistent action, a commitment to learning, and a willingness to refine and adapt your techniques as you grow.

This book is your partner in that journey. It will guide you every step of the way, providing practical strategies, encouragement, and a clear path to success. Your next sale begins with the confidence and skills you'll build right here. Let's get started!

Your Sales Skills Assessment & Evaluation Tool

Instructions: Evaluate your Sales Person based on the criteria listed below. Use the following scale to rate each criterion:
1 = Needs Improvement, 2 = Below Average, 3 = Average, 4 = Above Average, 5 = Excellent

Assessment Area	Criteria	Rating (1-5)
Attitude & Mindset	Self-Preparation: Grooming, Attitude, and Mindset	[ ]
	Inspires Confidence	[ ]
	Patience in Uncovering Needs	[ ]
Prospecting & Preparation	Prospecting Effectively with a System	[ ]
	Tracking Prospects	[ ]
	Thorough Preparation: Client, Market, Industry, Competition, Sales Tools	[ ]
Sales Process & Skills	Approaching Customers: Phone & In Person	[ ]
	Uncovering Needs	[ ]
	Asking the Right Questions	[ ]

Assessment Area	Criteria	Rating (1-5)
	Listening to Buyers	[ ]
	Picking Clues and Hints about Customer Needs	[ ]
	Note-Taking	[ ]
	Presenting Value and Proving Maximum ROI	[ ]
	Handling Objections with Grace	[ ]
	Cross and Up-Selling Opportunities	[ ]
	Able to Change Buyer Thinking and Inspire Them into Solutions that Matter	[ ]
	Proving That We Are the Best Choice over Competition	[ ]
	Building a Sense of Urgency to Initiate Action	[ ]
	Building Compelling Solutions	[ ]
	Effective Proposals and Presentations	[ ]
	Effectively Closing	[ ]
Post-Sales Engagement	Collaborating and Following Up Even After the Sales	[ ]

Total Score: ______ / 110

Overall Performance Level:
91-110: Excellent
71-90: Above Average
51-70: Average
31-50: Below Average
11-30: Needs Improvement

Evaluation Summary:

Areas of Excellence:

(List the criteria rated 4 or 5)

____
____
____
____
____
____
____
____
____
____

Areas for Improvement:

(List the criteria rated 1, 2, or 3)

____
____
____
____
____
____
____
____
____
____
____

Development Plan:

Identify specific actions, resources, or training needed to improve performance in areas rated below 3.

Understanding the Role of Self in Selling

The journey of becoming a top-notch sales professional begins with understanding yourself—your strengths, weaknesses, and the habits you need to develop to excel in your career. In this chapter, we'll take a deep dive into what creates satisfied customers, how you can embody the key attributes of successful salespeople, and how to master essential aspects like communication and making lasting impressions.

By the end of this chapter, you will have developed a clear understanding of how self-management, preparation, and attitude play a crucial role in your sales success. You'll also have practical tools and exercises to implement immediately, helping you refine and develop your approach to selling.

What Creates a Satisfied Customer?

At the heart of every successful sale is a satisfied customer. But satisfaction goes beyond simply delivering the product or service they purchased; it encompasses how you make them feel throughout the process. It starts from the very first interaction and continues through the entire sales cycle, including follow-ups.

To understand how to create a satisfied customer, consider these factors:

- ✓ Empathy: Understanding the customer's needs, concerns, and goals.
- ✓ Personalization: Tailoring your pitch and service to meet the specific needs of each customer.

- ✓ Trust: Establishing credibility and reliability so that customers feel secure in their decision to work with you.
- ✓ Follow-through: Delivering on promises and staying engaged post-sale.
- ✓ Problem-solving: Helping customers overcome challenges by presenting your solution in a way that addresses their pain points.
- ✓ When customers feel understood and valued, they are far more likely to be satisfied, which in turn leads to loyalty and referrals.

Reflection Exercise:

Think back to three customers you've interacted with in the past. In each case, analyze what made that customer satisfied or dissatisfied. Reflect on what you did to contribute to that satisfaction. Write a brief narrative for each experience, detailing:

- ✓ The customer's needs and concerns.
- ✓ How you addressed those needs.
- ✓ The outcome of the interaction.

Example: *"I once worked with a client who was hesitant about purchasing a large order due to budget constraints. I took the time to understand her concerns about cost and presented a customized solution that met her needs at a lower cost. In the end, not only did she make the purchase, but she also recommended me to another client. I realized that listening to her specific concerns and providing a tailored solution led to her satisfaction."*

Key Attributes of Top Sales Professionals and How to Imbibe Them

Successful sales professionals exhibit certain core attributes that set them apart. These attributes don't just appear overnight; they are cultivated through consistent effort, practice, and reflection. Let's explore some of these key attributes and how you can begin to incorporate them into your daily work:

- ✓ Resilience: Sales can be filled with rejections and setbacks, but top professionals bounce back quickly and persist in the face of challenges.
  How to develop it: Each time you face rejection, instead of seeing it as a failure, view it as an opportunity to learn. Keep a journal where you write down the objections you faced and brainstorm better ways to handle them next time.
- ✓ Empathy: The ability to understand and share the feelings of others is crucial in sales. When customers feel heard, they are more likely to trust you.
  How to develop it: Practice active listening in every conversation. Focus on understanding the customer's point of view before jumping in with your solution.
- ✓ Discipline: A structured and organized approach to work ensures consistent results.
  How to develop it: Start by creating a daily checklist of tasks. Prioritize your day with the most critical tasks at the top, such as prospecting and client follow-ups.
- ✓ Self-awareness: Knowing your strengths and weaknesses helps you improve where needed and leverage your strengths.
  How to develop it: Perform regular self-assessments, reflecting on your performance after each sales call or meeting.

The K.A.S.H. Framework: Keys to Success

The K.A.S.H. framework—Knowledge, Attitude, Skills, and Habits—forms the foundation of success in any profession, especially sales. Let's break it down:

- ✓ Knowledge: You must have a thorough understanding of your product or service, your market, industry, government regulations and your competitors- their strengths/ weaknesses- and how they compare with yours. Beyond this, you need to know your customer—their needs, challenges, and decision-making processes.

  Action Plan: Dedicate time each day to learning something new about your industry or your product. Subscribe to industry newsletters, read competitor websites, and keep updated on new features of your product.
- ✓ Attitude: A positive, confident attitude is essential in sales. Customers can sense hesitation or negativity, which can quickly turn them off.

  Action Plan: Start each day by setting a positive intention. Remind yourself why you are passionate about your product or service and how it benefits your customers.
- ✓ Skills: These include communication, negotiation, uncovering needs, selling solutions and value, closing techniques, and more. The more refined your skills, the more effectively you'll be able to close deals.

  Action Plan: Set weekly goals to practice a specific skill. For example, focus one week on improving your negotiation techniques by role-playing with a colleague or friend.

- ✓ Habits: Consistency is key in sales. Successful professionals develop daily habits that help them stay organized, focused, and productive.
  Action Plan: Identify the habits that will make the most impact, such as following up with prospects, tracking your sales pipeline, or dedicating time to prospecting. Create a habit tracker and stick to it for at least 21 days to make it a routine.

Self-Assessment Exercise:

Rate yourself on a scale of 1 to 5 for each element of the K.A.S.H. framework, with 1 being "needs improvement" and 5 being "highly proficient." Then, write down one action step you can take to improve in each area.

Communication and Influence (7:38:55 Rule)

Communication is one of the most important tools you have as a salesperson. The 7:38:55 rule is a well-known principle that states:

- ✓ 7% of communication is through the words we use.
- ✓ 38% is through tone of voice.
- ✓ 55% is through body language.

Understanding how communication breaks down helps you focus on more than just what you say. *Your tone and body language can either reinforce or undermine the message you're trying to convey.*

Exercise:

Take a few moments to reflect on your communication style. Break it down into three components:

- ✓ Words: How clear, concise, and meaningful are your words? Do you use jargon that might confuse your customers, or do you speak in terms they understand?
- ✓ Tone: Do you sound confident, friendly, and approachable? Or do you come across as unsure or robotic?
- ✓ Body Language: Are you open and welcoming with your posture? Do you make appropriate eye contact? Or do you cross your arms, avoid eye contact, or appear distracted?

Once you've analyzed these areas, ask a trusted colleague or friend to role-play with you and provide feedback on these three areas. Then, practice improving in the areas where you feel weakest.

Creating Lasting Impressions in 90 Seconds

The first 90 seconds of an interaction are crucial. Whether you're meeting someone for the first time or walking into a sales meeting, people make quick judgments. These initial impressions can have a lasting impact on whether or not you'll be successful. To make a strong first impression:

- ✓ Dress the part: Dress in a way that reflects professionalism and confidence.
- ✓ Smile: A genuine smile immediately puts people at ease.
- ✓ Be aware of your body language: Open posture, eye contact, and a firm handshake are key.
- ✓ Start with a positive, energetic greeting: Your energy sets the tone for the conversation.

Action Plan:

Prepare for your next sales meeting by creating a checklist for making a strong first impression. Use this checklist before every meeting:

- ✓ Are you dressed appropriately for the occasion?
- ✓ Do you have a genuine smile ready?
- ✓ Is your posture open and confident?
- ✓ Have you prepared a warm and energetic greeting?

Selling Yourself First

Before you can sell any product or service, you must first sell yourself. Customers need to believe in you before they believe in what you're offering. This is where personal credibility comes in.

Building personal credibility involves:

- ✓ Being authentic: Be yourself and show genuine interest in your customers.
- ✓ Following through on promises: Reliability is key in building trust.
- ✓ Building expertise: Customers are more likely to trust someone who is knowledgeable.

Exercise:

Write a personal sales pitch for yourself. Imagine you're selling YOU as a service. What are your strengths? What value do you bring to your customers? Keep your pitch under 60 seconds and practice delivering it with confidence.

Example: *"My name is [Your Name], and I specialize in helping businesses like yours find solutions that streamline operations and increase profitability. With over five years of experience in the industry and a commitment to understanding your unique challenges, I'm confident I can offer you strategies that will make a lasting impact."*

By completing these exercises, you will have taken the first critical steps towards understanding and mastering the role of self in selling. You'll be equipped with the personal attributes, knowledge, and strategies to build strong customer relationships and drive success in your sales career.

Planning Your Day and Activities

The second step to becoming a highly effective sales professional is learning to plan your day and activities. Successful salespeople know that managing their time and activities is key to maintaining productivity and reaching their goals. In this chapter, you will be guided through the essential skills for organizing your day, focusing on high-value activities, and optimizing your approach to prospecting and generating leads. The core activities of a professional salesperson revolve around four key areas: Planning, Prospecting, Selling, and Administration. Each of these plays a crucial role, but their time allocation should be strategically managed for maximum success.

By the end of this chapter, you will have a structured plan to manage your time efficiently, focus on revenue-generating tasks, and approach prospecting with clarity and confidence.

Managing Yourself and Your Day

Sales success is as much about managing your time as it is about managing relationships. Each day comes with competing priorities: prospecting, meetings, follow-ups, administrative work, and more. The key to staying productive is organizing your day to ensure that you focus on the activities that will generate the most revenue.

Begin by breaking down your day into manageable parts. The most effective salespeople schedule their day with a clear sense of purpose, ensuring that the majority of their time is spent on high-impact tasks, such as prospecting and selling.

The Four Key Activities for Sales Success

1. **Planning**

Planning involves both long-term and short-term preparation. Long-term planning helps set sales goals, while short-term planning ensures effective preparation for meetings and client interactions. Planning is essential for strategic thinking but should not consume too much time. It is important to find a balance and avoid over-planning, as this can take away from time spent on revenue-generating activities.

2. **Prospecting**

Prospecting refers to identifying new business opportunities and reaching out to potential clients to secure meetings. This is the lifeblood of the sales pipeline. To ensure future business, around 55% of your time should be dedicated to prospecting. Consistent prospecting ensures you have a healthy pipeline of leads to convert into customers. Without this, the pipeline dries up, leaving you with no future prospects to engage.

3. **Selling**

Selling involves direct, face-to-face interactions with customers, identifying their needs, and providing solutions. Approximately 25% of your time should be dedicated to selling. These efforts are what convert prospects into actual customers, creating immediate revenue. Direct interaction with clients should always be prioritized when opportunities arise, as it is where a salesperson has the most influence.

4. **Administration**

Administrative tasks, such as logging sales activities, maintaining customer records, and preparing forecasts, are necessary but should be minimized. While important for tracking progress and refining strategies, administrative work should not take up more than 20% of your time, combined with planning activities (Point 1). Keeping these tasks streamlined allows for more time to be dedicated to prospecting and selling.

How to Organize Daily Sales Activities Effectively

Start by creating a simple but effective daily plan that covers your key tasks, including:

- ✓ Prospecting and lead generation
- ✓ Client meetings or presentations
- ✓ Follow-ups and relationship management
- ✓ Administrative tasks (reports, emails, etc.)

Your goal should be to prioritize activities that will move you closer to closing deals or building relationships with prospects.

Step-by-Step Guide to Organizing Your Day:

- ✓ Begin with Prospecting: Dedicate your first hours of the day to prospecting. This is when your energy and focus are highest, making it the best time to generate leads and reach out to new prospects.
- ✓ Client Meetings: If possible, schedule client meetings in the middle of the day. This allows you to focus your energy on critical relationship-building activities when both you and your clients are fully engaged.
- ✓ Follow-ups: Allocate time towards the end of the day for follow-up activities, such as sending emails, checking in with existing clients, or setting up future meetings.
- ✓ Admin Tasks: Set aside the last part of your day for administrative tasks, like filing reports, updating your CRM, or preparing for the next day.

The 80/20 Rule for Revenue Generators

The Pareto Principle, commonly known as the 80/20 Rule, suggests that 80% of your results come from 20% of your efforts. In sales, this principle can help you maximize productivity by focusing your time and energy on the activities that generate the most revenue—**primarily** prospecting and selling.

Many sales professionals get bogged down by administrative tasks, meetings, and other non-revenue-generating activities. While these tasks are necessary, they should not dominate your day. To become more effective, you should spend 80% of your time prospecting and selling, and only 20% on other activities.

Focusing 80% of Time on Prospecting and Selling

To apply the 80/20 rule effectively, first take a close look at how you spend your time. Track your activities over a week, and at the end of the week, assess how much time was spent on high-value tasks (prospecting, selling) versus lower-value tasks (emails, admin work).

Daily Planner Template: Scheduling Key Activities

To help you get started, here's an example of a daily planner:

Time	Activity	Description
8:00 AM	Prospecting	Cold calls, emails, LinkedIn outreach
10:00 AM	Follow-up Calls/Emails	Reconnect with prospects and clients
11:00 AM	Client Meetings/Presentations	Face-to-face or virtual meetings
1:00 PM	Lunch and Recharge	Use this time to refresh and refocus
2:00 PM	Lead Research/Prospecting	Research potential clients or revisit cold leads
4:00 PM	Admin/Reports	Update CRM, fill out sales reports, schedule follow-ups
5:00 PM	Wrap-up	Review the day's work, prepare for tomorrow

Time Tracking Tool: Record Your Daily Activities for a Week

Here's a practical exercise to evaluate how well your current routine aligns with the 80/20 rule:

Step-by-Step Time Tracking Exercise:

- ✓ Record Activities: For one week, write down every task you perform during your workday, noting how much time you spent on each task.
- ✓ Categorize: Once you've tracked your activities, categorize them into two groups: Revenue-Generating Activities (prospecting, client calls, closing deals) and Non-Revenue-Generating Activities (admin, emails, meetings).
- ✓ Analyze: Add up the total hours spent on revenue-generating activities versus non-revenue-generating activities. The goal is to ensure that at least 80% of your time is focused on the former.
- ✓ Adjust: If less than 80% of your time is spent on prospecting and selling, adjust your schedule accordingly. Identify areas where you can delegate or streamline non-revenue tasks, such as automating reports or limiting time spent on emails.

A professional salesperson must recognize that their primary role is to generate revenue. By managing your time effectively—dedicating most of it to prospecting and selling while limiting planning and administrative tasks—you can maximize your productivity, stay ahead of competitors, and drive growth.

Prospecting & Generating Leads

Prospecting is the lifeblood of sales. Without a steady stream of leads, it's impossible to close deals and grow your sales pipeline. Generating leads requires a combination of creativity, persistence, and strategic thinking. There are many avenues for finding potential customers, from cold calling and email outreach to networking and social media.
Understanding the importance of prospecting and having a solid strategy in place can help you consistently find and nurture new leads.

Importance of Prospecting
Prospecting is vital because it allows you to build a pipeline of potential customers. Without it, you'll find yourself with nothing to sell, even if you have a great product or service. Regularly prospecting ensures that you always have potential clients in the pipeline, which in turn leads to consistent revenue generation.

How to Generate Leads and Track Them
There are various methods for generating leads. Some of the most common include:

- ✓ Cold calling: Reaching out to potential customers by phone.
- ✓ Email outreach: Sending targeted emails to prospects.
- ✓ Social media: Using platforms like LinkedIn to connect with potential clients.
- ✓ Networking: Attending industry events and building relationships with people who might be interested in your product.

- ✓ Referrals: Asking satisfied customers to refer you to others who might benefit from your services.

Once you have a steady flow of leads, it's essential to track them properly. Use a CRM (Customer Relationship Management) tool to keep track of every interaction you have with a lead, from the initial outreach to follow-ups and sales closures.

Step-by-Step Guide to Lead Tracking:

- ✓ Input new leads into your CRM: Each time you connect with a potential customer, input their contact information and notes about the conversation into your CRM.
- ✓ Set follow-up reminders: After each conversation, set a reminder to follow up in a specific time frame (e.g., 3 days, 1 week).
- ✓ Update regularly: Keep your CRM up to date with the latest information, including customer needs, preferences, and pain points.
- ✓ Move prospects through the pipeline: As prospects show more interest, move them through your sales pipeline toward the closing stage.

How to Identify and Qualify Prospects

Not every lead is worth pursuing. It's essential to identify and qualify prospects to ensure that you're focusing on those most likely to convert into paying customers. Qualifying prospects involves evaluating whether a lead has the potential to become a customer based on factors like their need for your product, their budget, and their decision-making authority.

Techniques for Finding Potential Clients

To identify the right prospects, follow these steps:

- ✓ Define your ideal customer: Start by creating a profile of your ideal customer. This profile should include demographic information (age, industry, location) as well as behavioral traits (buying habits, needs, and challenges).
- ✓ Research potential prospects: Use tools like LinkedIn, industry directories, and company websites to research potential clients that match your ideal customer profile.
- ✓ Use referrals and networking: Tap into your existing network for referrals. Referrals from satisfied customers are one of the most effective ways to find high-quality leads.
- ✓ Cold outreach: If you don't have warm leads to pursue, consider cold calling or cold emailing. While these methods may have lower conversion rates, they can still yield valuable prospects if done correctly.

Prospecting Worksheet: List 10 Prospects and Their Potential Needs

To practice identifying and qualifying prospects, complete the following exercise:

Step-by-Step Prospecting Exercise:

- ✓ List 10 potential prospects that fit your ideal customer profile. For each prospect, include the company name, contact information, and any relevant notes.
- ✓ Identify their potential needs. Based on your research, write down what you think their main pain points or challenges are. How can your product or service help solve those problems?
- ✓ Qualify the prospects. For each prospect, answer these key questions:
- ✓ Do they have a need for your product/service?

- ✓ Do they have the budget to purchase it?
- ✓ Are they the decision-maker or can they influence the decision?
- ✓ Example:
- ✓ Prospect: ACME Corporation Contact: John Doe, Director of Operations Potential Needs: Streamlining their supply chain operations Qualification: Yes, they have a need for our logistics software, and John is the key decision-maker.

By completing this worksheet, you'll have a list of qualified prospects ready to reach out to, along with a clear understanding of their needs.

Planning your day and activities effectively is the foundation of a successful sales career. By following the strategies outlined in this chapter, you can ensure that you focus on the tasks that will move the needle—prospecting, selling, and nurturing leads—while managing your time efficiently.

The Fundamentals of Selling

Selling is often misunderstood as simply convincing someone to buy a product or service. However, the most successful salespeople understand that selling is, at its core, a form of problem-solving. Your goal is not to push a product onto a customer, but to understand their needs, recognize their challenges, and offer solutions that improve their situation. When approached this way, selling becomes a collaborative process where both you and the customer are working toward a common goal: solving a problem.

This chapter will guide you through a structured, step-by-step sales process, helping you to reframe your approach to selling and master the fundamentals needed to succeed. By the end, you'll have a clear understanding of how to sell through problem-solving, as well as a six-step sales plan that can be implemented in any situation.

Selling as Problem-Solving

One of the most important shifts you can make as a salesperson is to stop thinking about selling as a transaction. Instead, approach every interaction as an opportunity to solve a problem for your customer. When you sell a product or service, what you are really doing is offering a solution that meets a specific need. This approach will not only help you build stronger relationships with your clients, but it will also make you more effective in closing deals.

Customers don't buy products—they buy solutions to their problems. Whether they need to save time, reduce costs, improve efficiency, or achieve personal satisfaction, the solution you provide is what will drive the sale. Your role as a salesperson is to understand their needs, show empathy for their challenges, and position your product or service as the ideal solution. Let's break this down into a practical exercise that will help you internalize the concept of selling as problem-solving.

Problem-Solving Worksheet: Identifying Common Problems Faced by Customers

In order to sell effectively, you need to anticipate the types of problems your potential customers might be facing. Think about your industry, the products or services you offer, and the types of clients you typically work with. What challenges are they dealing with on a regular basis? What problems keep them up at night?

Here is a step-by-step guide to help you complete the Problem-Solving Worksheet:

- ✓ Step 1: Brainstorm Customer Problems Begin by listing the most common problems your clients face. If you're unsure, think about the challenges that your product or service is designed to address. For example, if you sell a software product, your clients might be struggling with inefficiency, manual work processes, or outdated technology. If you sell insurance, your customers might be worried about risk or financial security.

  Example:

- Customers struggle with complex supply chains.
- Clients need a more cost-effective way to manage inventory.
- Customers worry about compliance with new regulations.

- ✓ Step 2: Identify the Root Cause of Each Problem For each problem you've listed, think about the root cause. Is the problem caused by a lack of resources? A lack of knowledge or expertise? Or perhaps by changes in the market that have made old solutions ineffective?

  Example:
- Root Cause: Inefficient systems lead to delays in the supply chain.
- Root Cause: Customers lack access to technology that streamlines inventory management.
- Root Cause: New regulations are complex and hard to understand without expert guidance.
- ✓ Step 3: Match Your Product or Service to the Problem Now, think about how your product or service can address these problems. What specific features or benefits make your offering the ideal solution?

  Example:
- Solution: Our logistics software simplifies supply chain management, reduces delays, and increases efficiency.
- Solution: Our cloud-based inventory system allows customers to track inventory in real time, cutting costs by 25%.
- Solution: Our consultancy service helps businesses navigate new regulations with expert support and compliance tools.
- ✓ Step 4: Write a Clear Solution Statement Once you've identified the problem, the root cause, and how your product or service solves it, write a concise statement that describes

this solution. This statement will help you communicate the value of your offering to the customer.

✓ Example Solution Statement:

- *"Our logistics software is designed to solve the problem of supply chain delays by automating key processes and providing real-time visibility, ensuring faster delivery times and increased efficiency."*
- *"Our cloud-based inventory system solves the problem of manual inventory tracking, allowing businesses to save time and reduce costs with real-time data."*

By the end of this exercise, you'll have a clear understanding of the problems your clients face, their root causes, and how your product or service can help solve them. This will help you position yourself as a problem-solver and give you the confidence to approach sales with a customer-centric mindset.

The 6-Step Selling Plan

Now that you understand how to reframe selling as problem-solving, let's look at the step-by-step process you can follow to close more deals. The 6-step selling plan is a structured approach to sales that guides you through each stage of the sales process, from identifying prospects to closing the deal. By following this plan, you'll ensure that every sales opportunity is approached in a methodical, professional way.

Step 1: Prospecting

The first step in the sales process is identifying potential customers, or prospects. These are individuals or businesses that might benefit from your product or service. Effective prospecting involves research, outreach, and relationship building.

Example: Imagine you sell marketing software. You might begin by identifying companies in your area that have recently launched new products and might need help with their marketing efforts. You could use LinkedIn or industry directories to find potential contacts at these companies.

Step 2: Qualifying

Once you've identified potential prospects, the next step is to qualify them. This means determining whether they are a good fit for your product or service, and whether they have the need, budget, and authority to make a purchase.

Example: After identifying a company that has recently launched a new product, you reach out to the marketing director and learn that they are actively seeking a new marketing software platform to improve their online campaigns. You confirm that they have the budget to invest in a solution like yours.

Step 3: Approach

With your qualified prospect in hand, it's time to approach them directly. This can be done via phone, email, or in person. The goal of the approach is to make a strong first impression and set the stage for a deeper conversation about how you can help solve their problem.

Example: You send an introductory email to the marketing director, explaining how your software has helped similar companies increase their online reach by 30%. You offer to set up a meeting to discuss how you can help their team achieve similar results.

Step 4: Presentation

Once you've made initial contact and the prospect has shown interest, it's time to uncover opportunities- their needs/ pain and only then present your solution. This is your opportunity to showcase how your product or service solves the client's specific problem, using the insights you gathered in the qualifying stage.

Example: During the meeting with the marketing director, you uncover a specific opportunity to present a detailed demo of your software, highlighting features that are specifically relevant to their needs. You show how the software can streamline their online campaigns, improve targeting, and increase conversions.

Step 5: Handling Objections

After your presentation, the prospect may have questions or concerns. This is natural, and it's important to be prepared to handle objections. Common objections might include concerns about cost, implementation, or whether your product is the right fit for their needs.

Example: The marketing director expresses concern about the cost of the software. You acknowledge their concern and explain how the software's ability to improve campaign efficiency will result in cost savings over time. You also offer a flexible payment plan to make the investment more manageable.

Step 6: Closing the Deal

The final step in the sales process is closing the deal. This is when you ask the prospect to make a commitment to purchase your product or service. There are many different closing techniques, from direct asks to more subtle approaches like trial closes.

Example: You follow up with the marketing director after the meeting and ask if they're ready to move forward with the purchase. They express interest but need approval from their finance team. You offer to send a detailed proposal outlining the benefits and ROI of the software, which helps them get the green light to move forward with the purchase.

Goal-Setting Exercise: Define Personal Objectives for Each Step

To help you internalize the 6-step selling plan, take some time to define personal objectives for each stage. This will help you stay focused and ensure that you're working toward specific outcomes at each step of the sales process.

Step-by-Step Guide to the Goal-Setting Exercise:

- ✓ Step 1: Prospecting Goal Set a goal for the number of new prospects you want to identify each week. This might involve researching leads, attending networking events, or asking for referrals.
  Example Goal: *"I will identify 10 new prospects each week by researching companies in my target industry and reaching out via email or LinkedIn."*
- ✓ Step 2: Qualifying Goal Define how many of your prospects you plan to qualify as high-potential leads. This involves asking the right questions to determine whether they have the need, budget, and decision-making authority.
  Example Goal: *"I will qualify at least 5 of my prospects each week by asking targeted questions about their needs, budget, and decision-making process."*

- ✓ Step 3: Approach Goal Set a goal for how many initial outreach attempts you will make to qualified prospects each week.
  Example Goal: *"I will make initial contact with at least 7 qualified prospects each week through phone calls, emails, or in-person meetings."*
- ✓ Step 4: Presentation Goal Decide how many presentations or product demos you will aim to deliver each week.
  Example Goal: *"I will visit/ call- uncover customer's needs, present my solution to 3 prospects each week, tailoring my pitch to address their specific problems/ needs."*
- ✓ Step 5: Handling Objections Goal Prepare yourself for common objections by setting a goal to handle at least 1 objection during each presentation or sales call.
  Example Goal: *"During each presentation, I will anticipate and address at least 1 potential objection, such as cost or implementation concerns."*
- ✓ Step 6: Closing Goal Finally, set a goal for how many deals you will aim to close each month.
  Example Goal: *"I will close at least 3 deals each month by following up with prospects, sending proposals, and asking for the sale."*

By defining clear objectives for each step, you'll be able to track your progress and stay motivated throughout the sales process. Each goal will help you move closer to closing more deals and achieving greater success as a problem-solving salesperson.

Preparation for Success

Success in sales starts long before you ever meet with a prospect. The key to effective selling lies in preparation—mental, physical, and tactical. A well-prepared salesperson not only understands their product or service but also knows their customer, industry, and competition inside out. This chapter is about ensuring that when you engage with a prospect, you're ready to present yourself as a confident, knowledgeable, and solution-oriented professional.

In this chapter, we will walk through how to prepare for success, focusing on self-preparation, understanding your customer, and conducting in-depth industry and competitive analysis. We will also review the tools you need to streamline your sales process. By the end of this chapter, you will have a clear, step-by-step plan to ensure you're fully prepared for every sales interaction, setting yourself up for consistent success.

Self-Preparation: Building Confidence

Before you can sell effectively to others, you need to be confident in yourself. Confidence is built through preparation, practice, and the right mindset. It's about being mentally and physically ready to take on each day's challenges. The way you start your day has a significant impact on how you approach your work, and developing a routine that energizes you will set the tone for success.

The Importance of Mental and Physical Readiness

Mental readiness means having a clear, focused mind. It's about starting each day with the right attitude, free from distractions or anxieties. Physical readiness means taking care of your body to ensure you have the energy and stamina to engage with prospects throughout the day. Together, mental and physical readiness create a strong foundation for confidence.

To help you build confidence, follow this Morning Routine Checklist to ensure you start each day with intention and purpose:

- ✓ Morning Routine Checklist: Create Your Daily Preparation Routine
- ✓ Wake up Early: Successful salespeople start their day early, giving themselves enough time to prepare mentally and physically. Set your alarm at least an hour before you need to start working to allow time for self-care.
  Example: If you typically start your day at 8 AM, wake up at 6:30 AM to give yourself enough time for a peaceful, focused morning routine.
- ✓ Practice Gratitude: Before diving into your day, take a few moments to reflect on what you're grateful for. Gratitude shifts your focus to positive thoughts and sets a constructive tone for the day.
  Example: Write down three things you're grateful for each morning, such as your family, your health, or a recent success at work.
- ✓ Set Daily Goals: Establishing clear objectives for the day helps you stay focused and productive. Set both professional and personal goals each morning, whether it's completing a set number of prospect calls or taking time for a workout.

Example: *"Today, I will contact 5 new prospects, prepare for an upcoming sales presentation, and go for a 30-minute walk after lunch."*

- ✓ Engage in Physical Exercise: A short workout can energize your body and improve mental clarity. Even 15–20 minutes of physical activity can make a big difference in how you approach the day.
  Example: Incorporate a quick home workout, stretching routine, or a brisk walk into your morning to get your blood flowing and clear your mind.
- ✓ Review Your Schedule: Take time each morning to review your daily schedule. Know which meetings, calls, or tasks you have lined up and mentally prepare for them.
  Example: *"At 10 AM, I have a call with a potential client. I'll review their background and prepare for any questions they might have about our services."*
- ✓ Affirm Your Abilities: Confidence is often reinforced by reminding yourself of your skills and abilities. Use positive affirmations to build your self-esteem.
  Example: Say to yourself, *"I am well-prepared, knowledgeable, and ready to make a positive impact in my sales conversations today."*

This morning routine will help ensure that you start each day prepared, both mentally and physically, giving you the confidence needed to face any sales challenge.

Understanding Your Customer

The second part of preparation involves deeply understanding your customer. Before you meet with a prospect, it's critical to know who they are, what their needs are, and what pain points they are experiencing. By taking the time to understand your customer's world, you'll be better positioned to offer them a solution that directly addresses their specific challenges.

Researching Customer Needs, Pain Points, and Desires

To effectively sell to a customer, you need to know what motivates them to make decisions. This means understanding their needs, the problems they are trying to solve, and the goals they are working toward. By aligning your product or service with their desires, you can position yourself as a valuable problem-solver, not just a salesperson.

Here's how to research and analyze your target customers:

- ✓ Identify Your Customer Segment: Start by defining who your ideal customers are. What industry are they in? What is their role? Are they decision-makers? Understanding your audience allows you to tailor your approach to their specific needs.

  Example: If you're selling software, your ideal customer might be the IT manager of a medium-sized company looking for ways to improve workflow efficiency.
- ✓ Investigate Their Pain Points: Look for common challenges faced by customers in your industry. What problems are they looking to solve? This could be gathered through

online research, industry reports, or directly by asking current clients.
Example: *"My customers are struggling with outdated technology that leads to inefficient processes and higher costs."*

- ✓ Understand Their Desires: Beyond solving problems, customers also have aspirations and goals. Understand what they want to achieve—whether it's increasing revenue, expanding their business, or improving customer satisfaction.
Example: *"My customers want to streamline their operations to increase productivity and reduce operational costs."*

With this understanding, you can craft your pitch to address both their pain points and their desires, making your product or service an irresistible solution.

Customer Profile Template: Develop a Sample Profile for Your Target Customer

To help organize this information, use the following customer profile template. Fill it out for each type of customer you plan to engage with, so you are prepared when meeting prospects.

- ✓ Customer Name: [Company/Individual]
- ✓ Industry: [Industry or Sector]
- ✓ Job Role: [Their Position]
- ✓ Key Pain Points: [What problems are they facing?]
- ✓ Goals/Desires: [What are they trying to achieve?]
- ✓ How We Can Help: [What solutions can you offer to address their needs?]

For example:

- ✓ Customer Name: ABC Manufacturing
- ✓ Industry: Manufacturing
- ✓ Job Role: Operations Manager
- ✓ Key Pain Points: Outdated equipment is causing production delays.
- ✓ Goals/Desires: Wants to improve production efficiency and lower costs.
- ✓ How We Can Help: Offer a modern production management system that reduces downtime and increases output.

Industry, Market, and Competition Analysis

Understanding your customer is only part of the equation. To prepare for success in sales, you also need to be knowledgeable about your industry, the market you operate in, and your competition. This will enable you to speak intelligently about trends, anticipate objections, and position your product or service in a way that stands out.

Key Factors to Research About Your Industry and Competitors

- ✓ Industry Trends: Stay up-to-date with changes in your industry. What innovations are happening? Are there new regulations or market shifts that could impact your customers' decision-making?
  Example: If you sell medical equipment, you should be aware of the latest advancements in healthcare technology and how new regulations affect purchasing decisions.
- ✓ Market Dynamics: Understand the overall state of the market you're selling into. Is it growing or shrinking? Are there external factors like economic conditions or

technological changes affecting buyer behavior?
Example: If you're selling in the software industry, know how the rise of cloud computing is affecting on-premise software sales and how you can leverage this shift in your conversations with prospects.

- ✓ Competitor Offerings: Know who your competitors are and what they offer. What are their strengths and weaknesses? How does your product or service compare? Being able to differentiate yourself from competitors is crucial to convincing customers to choose you.
Example: If a competitor offers a similar product at a lower price, your advantage might be better customer support or additional features that justify the higher cost.

Competitive Analysis Worksheet: List Competitors and How You Compare

To help you organize your competitive analysis, fill out the following worksheet. Compare your company's offerings to your competitors' and identify areas where you can differentiate yourself.

- ✓ Competitor Name: [Name of Competitor]
- ✓ Product/Service: [What do they offer?]
- ✓ Strengths: [What are their advantages?]
- ✓ Weaknesses: [Where are they lacking?]
- ✓ How We Compare: [How does your product/service differ?]

For example:

- ✓ Competitor Name: XYZ Solutions
- ✓ Product/Service: Project management software

- ✓ Strengths: Lower price, easy-to-use interface
- ✓ Weaknesses: Limited customization, no customer support
- ✓ How We Compare: Our software offers full customization options and 24/7 support, making it ideal for businesses with complex needs.

Sales Tools and Strategy

Having the right tools and strategies in place can make your sales process more efficient and effective. In today's competitive environment, leveraging technology is a must. Customer relationship management (CRM) systems, presentation software, and other sales tools allow you to track your progress, streamline communications, and deliver polished presentations.

Choosing the Right Tools to Enhance Effectiveness

Sales tools are designed to make your life easier, but only if you use them correctly. Choosing the right tools that align with your sales strategy is key. Here's a step-by-step guide to evaluating and implementing the right tools for your sales process:

- ✓ Identify What You Need: What specific needs do you have in your sales process? Do you need a tool to track customer interactions? A presentation tool for demos? Identifying the pain points in your workflow will help you choose the right tools.

  Example: If you struggle to keep track of client communications, a CRM tool like Salesforce or HubSpot could help you manage leads and follow-ups.

- ✓ Research Options: Look for tools that align with your needs. Compare features, pricing, and ease of use. Choose tools that are scalable and adaptable as your business grows.
  Example: If you frequently present to clients, research options for presentation software like PowerPoint, Google Slides, or Canva for creating visually appealing decks.
- ✓ Implement and Integrate: Once you've selected your tools, take time to learn how to use them properly. Integrate them into your daily routine and ensure they work seamlessly with your existing workflow.
  Example: Set up your CRM to automatically send follow-up emails after each sales call, saving you time and ensuring you never miss a follow-up.

Tools Checklist: List and Rate the Effectiveness of Your Current Tools

To assess whether your current tools are serving you well, use the following checklist to evaluate their effectiveness:

- ✓ Tool Name: [CRM, Presentation Software, etc.]
- ✓ Purpose: [What does it help you do?]
- ✓ Rating: [On a scale of 1-10, how effective is this tool?]
- ✓ Comments: [Are there any limitations or areas for improvement?]

For example:

- ✓ Tool Name: Salesforce
- ✓ Purpose: CRM for managing leads and customer interactions

- ✓ Rating: 9/10
- ✓ Comments: Very effective for tracking customer communications, but can be complex to use for beginners.

By evaluating your tools regularly, you can ensure you're using the best possible resources to support your sales efforts.

In conclusion, preparation is the key to successful selling. By focusing on self-preparation, understanding your customer, researching your industry and competition, and leveraging the right tools, you will set yourself up for success in every sales interaction. Take the time to complete the exercises in this chapter, and you will be well on your way to becoming a confident, knowledgeable, and prepared salesperson ready to tackle any challenge that comes your way.

Approaching Your Customers

Mastering the art of approaching customers is the foundation of any successful sales career. The initial contact sets the tone for everything that follows. A strong approach can build rapport and open the door to meaningful conversations, while a weak one may leave your prospect uninterested or disengaged. Whether you are making a cold call, reaching out through email, or meeting someone in person, the way you introduce yourself matters. This chapter will guide you through the essential steps to confidently approach customers, structuring your introduction for maximum impact and crafting a powerful elevator pitch that gets your message across in a clear and compelling manner.

The Art of the Approach: First Contact

Making the first contact with a potential customer is a critical moment in the sales process. How you approach this moment can make or break the opportunity. The goal is to make a strong first impression, capture the prospect's attention, and set the stage for further engagement. To do this effectively, you must structure your introduction thoughtfully, ensuring that it is clear, concise, and impactful.

Let's break down how to make a successful first approach by focusing on the following components: Salutation, Name, Company, and Purpose. Each component serves a specific role in shaping the overall tone and content of your introduction.

Structuring Your Introduction for Maximum Impact

- ✓ Salutation: Setting the Tone

  Your salutation is the first thing the customer hears, so it's important to get it right. Whether you're calling, emailing, or meeting in person, a polite and professional greeting sets the tone for the conversation. In a phone or face-to-face interaction, you might say, *"Good morning" or "Good afternoon,"* depending on the time of day. If you're communicating via email, a simple *"Hello" or "Hi* [Customer's Name]" is often best.

  Example: If you're calling a business professional, you might begin with: *"Good morning, this is Alex from Evergreen Solutions. May I speak with Ms. Taylor, please?"*

  In an email, your greeting might be: *"Hi Ms. Taylor, I hope this message finds you well."*

- ✓ Name: Personalizing the Conversation

  Using the prospect's name makes the interaction feel more personal and engaging. Always ensure you know how to pronounce the person's name correctly, and be mindful of their preferred title (Mr., Ms., Dr., etc.). This shows respect and professionalism.

  Example: If you're speaking to Dr. Maria Robinson, begin your introduction with: *"Good afternoon, Dr. Robinson. My name is Alex Parker with Evergreen Solutions."*

  If you're emailing, use their name right after your salutation:

"Hi Dr. Robinson, I hope you're having a great day."

- ✓ Company: Establishing Credibility

  After the salutation and name, introduce your company. This gives the prospect context about who you are and why you are reaching out. When stating your company name, do so with confidence, as it reflects your belief in your company's value. If your company is well-known in the industry, mentioning its reputation can work in your favor.

  Example*: "Good afternoon, Dr. Robinson. My name is Alex Parker, and I represent Evergreen Solutions. We specialize in streamlining business processes for healthcare providers across the region."*

- ✓ Purpose: Creating a Connection

  Finally, you need to explain the purpose of your approach. Keep this part concise, focusing on how you can potentially solve a problem or provide value. The goal is to pique the prospect's interest, not overwhelm them with too much information upfront. At this stage, you are simply introducing a potential solution, not diving into a full sales pitch.

  Example: "*Good afternoon, Dr. Robinson. My name is Alex Parker, and I represent Evergreen Solutions. We specialize in streamlining business processes for healthcare providers across the region. I'm reaching out today because I believe our software could help your practice reduce paperwork and improve patient satisfaction."*

Approach Script Template: Write and Refine Your Introduction

Now that you understand the key elements of a great introduction, it's time to create your own approach script. Your script will serve as a template that you can adapt depending on the customer and context. The goal is to keep your message clear, direct, and professional while leaving room for flexibility so you can tailor your introduction to different prospects.

Here's a step-by-step guide to writing and refining your introduction:

- ✓ Step 1: Draft Your Salutation and Name Begin with a friendly greeting, followed by the customer's name and your name. Make sure the tone is warm and professional. If you're emailing, include a personalized detail such as *"I hope your week is going well."*
  Example: *"Good afternoon, Ms. Taylor. My name is Alex Parker, and I'm with Evergreen Solutions."*
- ✓ Step 2: Introduce Your Company After introducing yourself, provide a brief description of your company, making sure to highlight what makes your business stand out. Keep it simple but meaningful.
  Example: *"Evergreen Solutions is known for helping small businesses streamline their operations using customized software solutions."*
- ✓ Step 3: State Your Purpose Next, explain why you're reaching out. This should be brief and focused on the customer's potential needs, not your product's features.
  Example: *"I'm reaching out because I believe our software could help you reduce operating*

costs and improve efficiency in managing your supply chain."

- ✓ Step 4: Craft Your Call-to-Action End your approach with a clear next step, such as scheduling a call or sending more information. Keep this light and respectful of the prospect's time.
  Example: *"I'd love the opportunity to discuss how we could support your business. Would you be open to a brief call this week?"*
- ✓ Step 5: Practice and Refine Practice your approach out loud, either on your own or with a colleague. Pay attention to your tone and pace, making sure your introduction feels natural and confident. Refine any awkward phrasing and adjust as needed for different scenarios.

Your Elevator Pitch

Once you've made initial contact and captured your prospect's attention, it's time to deliver your elevator pitch. An elevator pitch is a concise, persuasive summary of your company and its value. The goal is to communicate who you are, what you do, and why it matters—all in the span of about 30 seconds (roughly the length of an elevator ride). A well-crafted elevator pitch can quickly engage a prospect and prompt them to want to learn more.

The key to crafting an effective elevator pitch is clarity. You want to be straightforward while conveying enthusiasm and confidence. Your pitch should be adaptable so that you can tweak it depending on who you're talking to and the situation you're in.

Crafting a Concise, Impactful Pitch

Your elevator pitch needs to pack a punch, and to do that, it must be clear, concise, and focused on the prospect's needs. Here's how to build a compelling pitch:

- ✓ Step 1: Start with a Hook The hook is a sentence that grabs your listener's attention right away. You could ask a question or make a bold statement about a problem your customer likely faces. The goal is to engage them immediately.
  Example: *"Did you know that most businesses lose up to 20% of revenue due to inefficient supply chain management?"*
- ✓ Step 2: Introduce Your Solution Once you've captured their attention with your hook, introduce your company and the solution you offer. Keep it focused on the problem your prospect is facing and how you can help solve it.
  Example: *"At Evergreen Solutions, we specialize in supply chain optimization. Our software helps businesses like yours reduce operating costs by automating and streamlining processes."*
- ✓ Step 3: Highlight the Benefits After introducing your solution, explain the benefits of working with you. Focus on the tangible outcomes your prospect will experience—whether it's saving time, reducing costs, or increasing efficiency.
  Example: *"Our clients typically see a 15% reduction in operational costs within the first six months of implementing our system."*
- ✓ Step 4: End with a Call-to-Action Finish your pitch with a call-to-action. This could be asking

if they'd like to learn more, inviting them to a demo, or simply asking for a follow-up meeting.
Example: *"I'd love to show you how we can help your business achieve similar results. Would you be open to a brief conversation next week?"*

- ✓ Step 5: Rehearse Until It's Natural Like your approach, your elevator pitch should feel conversational, not rehearsed. Practice saying it aloud until it flows smoothly. You want to come across as confident and enthusiastic, not robotic.

Elevator Pitch Worksheet: Build and Rehearse Your Pitch

To help you craft and perfect your elevator pitch, complete the following worksheet. This will guide you through the process of refining each component of your pitch so that it's clear, concise, and impactful.

- ✓ Step 1: Write Your Hook
  Write a sentence that grabs attention, either by asking a question or making a bold statement.
  Example: *"Are you looking to reduce inefficiencies in your production process?"*
- ✓ *Step 2: Introduce Your Company and Solution*
  In one or two sentences, describe who you are and what your company does, focusing on the problem you solve.
  Example: *"At Evergreen Solutions, we provide manufacturing companies with customized software that streamlines their production workflows and reduces waste."*
- ✓ Step 3: Highlight the Benefits

Explain the main benefits of your solution. Be specific about the outcomes your customers typically experience.
Example: "*Our system has helped manufacturers decrease production time by 25%, significantly boosting their bottom line.*"

- ✓ Step 4: End with a Call-to-Action
  Write a sentence that invites the prospect to take the next step, such as scheduling a call or demo.
  Example: *"I'd love to show you how our system could do the same for your business. Can we set up a time to talk further?"*
- ✓ Step 5: Rehearse and Refine
  Once you've written your pitch, practice saying it aloud. Time yourself to ensure it fits within the 30-second timeframe. Adjust any awkward phrasing and continue refining until it feels natural and conversational.
- ✓ Example of Full Elevator Pitch:
  "Are you looking to reduce inefficiencies in your production process? At Evergreen Solutions, we provide manufacturing companies with customized software that streamlines their production workflows and reduces waste. Our system has helped manufacturers decrease production time by 25%, significantly boosting their bottom line. I'd love to show you how our system could do the same for your business. Can we set up a time to talk further?"

By following these steps and practicing regularly, you'll be able to confidently deliver your pitch in any situation, whether it's at a networking event, on a sales call, or during a casual conversation.

In conclusion, approaching customers with confidence and clarity is a skill that can be learned and perfected. Whether you're making an initial contact or delivering an elevator pitch, the key is to be prepared, know your audience, and communicate your message in a way that resonates with them. Through the exercises in this chapter, you will be able to craft compelling introductions and elevator pitches that leave a lasting impression and open the door to more meaningful sales conversations. Remember to practice, refine, and adapt your approach to suit each prospect and situation. With time and experience, you'll become a master at approaching customers and delivering a pitch that gets results.

Understanding the Buying Process

Sales is more than just presenting products or services and closing deals; it's about understanding the journey your customers take from identifying a need to making a purchase. This journey involves various stages, emotions, and decision-making processes that sales professionals must understand if they want to guide customers effectively toward making a purchase. To achieve success, you need to not only recognize what your customers want but also understand who the key players in the buying decision are and how they influence the process.

In this chapter, we will explore the customer buying process by focusing on their needs and desires, the stages they go through on their journey, and the types of buyers you will encounter. Through exercises and practical tools, you will learn how to map out the customer journey and identify key decision-makers, helping you align your sales approach with the customer's process and improve your chances of success.

Understanding Customer WANTS

At the core of any purchase lies a customer's wants and needs. While needs are often the foundational reason for a purchase, wants are the emotional drivers that influence customer behavior and ultimately guide decision-making. For instance, a company may need software to streamline operations, but what they *want* might be a system that is easy to use, customizable, and comes with outstanding customer service. It is crucial for sales professionals to understand not only what the

customer needs but also what they desire from a product or service. This understanding helps tailor your sales approach to address both practical and emotional factors.
The earlier you Qualify Customers **WANTS** it can help in many ways:

- ✓ **W** ants- exactly what are they looking for
- ✓ **A** uthorities- decision-making process- What level of influence do they have on making decisions?
- ✓ **N** eeds- of their organisational goals- Does the Prospect have a Need worth Solving?
- ✓ **T** imescales- of their evaluation and implementation- How soon they need a solution?
- ✓ **S** pend Capacity- Budget and when available- Do they have or can they find the ability to spend Money on solving these challenges?

To fully grasp what drives your customers, let's explore the key drivers behind customer purchases:
Key Drivers Behind Customer Purchases

- ✓ Solution to a Problem: Customers often purchase products or services to solve a specific problem they are facing. Identifying this problem is crucial for positioning your offering as the ideal solution.
  Example: A business struggling with slow internal communication may seek a software solution to streamline processes and improve collaboration. The key driver here is the need for efficiency.
- ✓ Desire for Improvement: Customers are often motivated by the desire to improve their current situation. Whether it's improving

productivity, reducing costs, or increasing convenience, this desire can drive purchasing decisions.
Example: A company may want to switch to more energy-efficient machinery not only to reduce operational costs but also to improve their environmental footprint.

- ✓ Emotional Satisfaction: Sometimes, purchases are driven by emotional desires, such as wanting to feel secure, in control, or recognized for making the right choice. Customers often seek products or services that align with these emotions.
  Example: A high-end consulting firm may not just want results but also a prestigious solution that reflects well on the company's status.
- ✓ Fear of Missing Out (FOMO): Customers are sometimes driven by a fear of missing out on a beneficial opportunity. This is particularly relevant in competitive industries where having the latest technology or most innovative solutions can be a competitive advantage.
  Example: A company may feel pressured to adopt new AI-driven solutions to keep pace with competitors and avoid falling behind.

Buyer Journey Mapping: Understanding the Stages

- ✓ Once you understand what motivates customers, it's time to map out the stages of their journey. The buyer's journey is the process that customers go through before making a purchase. It typically consists of the following stages: awareness, consideration, and decision. Let's break these down further.

- ✓ Awareness Stage: This is the stage where customers realize they have a problem or need. They are not yet sure what solutions exist but are actively researching their pain points.
  Example: A business might realize that they are losing clients due to poor customer service and begin researching ways to improve their customer support processes.
- ✓ Consideration Stage: During this stage, customers are aware of potential solutions and begin comparing different options. They will evaluate different products or services based on their needs, features, and cost-effectiveness.
  Example: The same business might start looking at different customer service software solutions, comparing features such as live chat support, automated responses, and integration with their existing systems.
- ✓ Decision Stage: This is the final stage where the customer decides which product or service to purchase. They are weighing all the pros and cons and might seek validation from other decision-makers or influencers in their organization before making the final call.
  Example: After evaluating various software options, the business narrows its choices to two and brings in the IT manager and customer service lead to discuss which option would best suit their operations.

Buyer Journey Mapping Template: Map Out a Typical Buyer's Journey

To help you understand the specific stages your customers go through, here is a step-by-step guide for mapping out a typical buyer's journey:

- ✓ Step 1: Identify the Customer Problem or Need Start by understanding the primary problem or need that leads customers to start the buying journey. What issue are they trying to solve, and how does it impact their business?

  Example: The problem is inefficient communication within the company, which is causing delays in project execution and client dissatisfaction.
- ✓ Step 2: Determine the Research Process Next, outline how your customers research their options. What sources of information do they turn to (e.g., online searches, referrals, reviews)? What are the factors they prioritize during this research stage?

  Example: The company researches solutions by reading online reviews, consulting colleagues in their industry, and attending webinars on improving business communication.
- ✓ Step 3: Identify the Consideration Factors In this step, note what your customer is likely considering as they compare different solutions. Are they looking at cost, ease of implementation, reliability, or something else?

  Example: The company is considering software options based on cost, integration with existing systems, and whether the software can be easily adopted by their team.

- ✓ Step 4: Outline the Decision-Making Process Who is involved in the final decision, and what are the deciding factors? Is there a hierarchy of decision-makers, and are other stakeholders influencing the choice?
  Example: The company's leadership team, along with the IT and HR departments, will make the final decision. Key factors include price, user-friendliness, and long-term scalability.

Types of Buyers and Their Roles

In many buying situations, multiple people are involved in the decision-making process. These individuals can play different roles within an organization, and understanding these roles is essential for navigating the sales process effectively. The main types of buyers typically fall into one of the following categories: decision-makers, influencers, gatekeepers, and users. Each plays a distinct role in the purchase process and may have different priorities and motivations.

Let's explore the various buyer roles and how you can identify and approach them.

- ✓ Decision-Makers: These are the individuals with the authority to make the final purchase decision. They often hold senior positions within the organization, such as the CEO, CFO, or department heads. Decision-makers are primarily concerned with how the purchase will impact the company as a whole, including financial implications and return on investment.
  Example: The CFO of a company may be the final decision-maker when it comes to

approving the purchase of a new enterprise resource planning (ERP) system.

- ✓ Influencers: Influencers are individuals who may not have the authority to make the final decision but can heavily influence it. They are often subject matter experts or senior employees who are consulted during the decision-making process.
  Example: The IT manager in a company may influence the decision of which software system to implement because they have technical expertise and understand the company's needs.
- ✓ Gatekeepers: Gatekeepers control access to decision-makers and can either facilitate or block your efforts to reach the key decision-makers. These are often executive assistants, office managers, or lower-level employees tasked with screening calls and emails.
  Example: The personal assistant of the CEO might serve as a gatekeeper, ensuring that only the most relevant sales pitches reach their boss's desk.
- ✓ Users: Users are the individuals who will interact with the product or service on a day-to-day basis. While they may not have the power to approve the purchase, their feedback and experiences often influence the final decision, especially when it comes to ease of use and functionality.
  Example: The employees in the HR department who will be using a new software system to manage payroll will likely provide input on how user-friendly they find the system during the evaluation phase.

Buyer Roles Worksheet: List Key Roles in a Typical Customer Organization

To help you identify the key players within a customer organization, use the following worksheet to outline the roles you may encounter and their potential influence on the purchase process. This will help you tailor your sales approach based on who you are interacting with and their specific concerns.

- ✓ Step 1: Identify the Decision-Maker Start by identifying who within the organization has the final authority to approve the purchase. This may be a single person or a committee.
  Example: In a mid-sized company, the final decision-maker may be the CFO, who oversees all major financial decisions.
- ✓ Step 2: List Potential Influencers Next, list the individuals who are likely to have a strong influence on the decision-making process. These could be department heads, technical experts, or consultants who are brought in to evaluate the solution.
  Example: The IT manager and head of operations are influencers who will evaluate the technical aspects of the solution and how it fits into the company's workflow.
- ✓ Step 3: Identify the Gatekeepers Determine who the gatekeepers are and consider how to effectively communicate with them to gain access to the decision-makers.
  Example: The executive assistant to the CEO is the gatekeeper. Building rapport with this individual may be key to securing a meeting with the CEO.

- ✓ Step 4: Consider the Users Finally, think about who the end-users of the product or service will be. Their feedback is crucial to ensuring that the solution you offer meets their practical needs.
  Example: The employees in the sales department will be using the software daily to track customer interactions and manage leads.

By understanding the customer buying process and identifying the key roles within the organization, you can better align your sales efforts with the customer's needs and decision-making framework. This not only enhances your ability to connect with customers but also helps build trust and credibility, leading to more successful and meaningful sales outcomes.

Uncovering Needs and Building Value

When working in sales, the key to success lies in uncovering the real needs of your prospects and building a value proposition that resonates with them. Without this understanding, it's challenging to present your product or service in a way that makes the prospect feel it's the right solution for them. This chapter will guide you through the process of gathering crucial information by asking effective questions, actively listening, and ultimately proving the value of your offering.

We will explore questioning techniques such as the 5Ws/1H approach and the C.O.R.K. model to uncover your prospect's needs. You'll also learn how to develop active listening skills and use the F.A.B. framework to prove the value of your product or service. Each section is supported by exercises that will help you implement these techniques step-by-step in real-life situations.

Effective Questioning Techniques

Asking the right questions is fundamental to uncovering the needs of your prospects. By understanding their challenges, goals, and pain points, you can better position your solution. In this section, we'll explore two questioning techniques: the 5Ws/1H framework and the C.O.R.K. model.

The 5Ws/1H Questioning Framework

The 5Ws/1H framework helps you explore different aspects of your prospect's situation. By asking questions that focus on "Who," "What," "When,"

"Where," "Why," and "How," you gather comprehensive information

Here's how you can use the 5Ws/1H:

- ✓ Who is involved in the decision-making process? This helps you identify the key stakeholders and influencers.
- ✓ What are the main challenges or issues your prospect is currently facing? This allows you to identify their primary pain points.
- ✓ When do they need to implement a solution? This gives you insight into the prospect's timeline and urgency.
- ✓ Where is the impact of these issues most felt? Knowing where the problem occurs helps you understand the scope of the challenge.
- ✓ Why is solving this problem important to them now? This helps uncover the motivations behind their need.
- ✓ How are they currently dealing with the problem? Understanding their current approach provides insights into their decision-making process.

For example, if you're selling a project management software:

- ✓ Who: "Who in your team is responsible for managing timelines and resources?"
- ✓ What: "What challenges do you face in ensuring project deadlines are met?"
- ✓ When: "When do you plan to implement a new project management system?"
- ✓ Where: "Where do delays tend to occur most frequently in your process?"
- ✓ Why: "Why is it important to improve your project timelines now?"

- ✓ How: "How are you currently managing your project schedules and updates?"

The C.O.R.K. Model of Questioning

The C.O.R.K. model provides a structure for guiding conversations toward uncovering a prospect's needs. This technique breaks down into four key areas:

- ✓ Current Circumstances: Start by asking about the prospect's current situation to understand where they are now.
  Example: "Can you describe your current process for managing customer inquiries?"
- ✓ Obstacles or Problem-Uncovering Questions: Ask about the problems they face to identify pain points.
  Example: "What challenges are you experiencing in keeping track of inquiries and follow-ups?"
- ✓ Repercussions or Impact of the Problem: Focus on the consequences of not addressing the problem. This helps your prospect understand the importance of finding a solution.
  Example: "What impact does delayed follow-up have on your customer satisfaction and sales?"
- ✓ Key for the Solution: Guide the conversation toward the solution, asking about what they would need in a new system or process. This sets the stage for positioning your product as the answer.
  Example: "What are the most important features you'd need in a solution to overcome these challenges?"

Exercise: Questioning Worksheet

To practice using these questioning techniques, follow these steps:

- ✓ Step 1: Select a current prospect or client for whom you're preparing to have a discovery meeting. Review their profile and try to anticipate their potential needs or challenges.
  Example: You are meeting with a medium-sized e-commerce company that is experiencing shipping delays.
- ✓ Step 2: Write three questions using the 5Ws/1H framework.
  "Who is responsible for managing your shipping and logistics operations?"
  "What are the main issues you're facing with your current shipping process?"
  "When do these shipping delays usually occur, and how do they affect your business?"
- ✓ Step 3: Write four questions using the C.O.R.K. model.
  Current Circumstances: *"Can you describe your current process for tracking and managing shipments?"*
  Obstacles: *"What challenges are you facing in ensuring timely deliveries?"*
  Repercussions: *"How are these delays affecting customer satisfaction and repeat business?"*
  Key for the Solution: *"What would an ideal solution look like for you in terms of improving your shipping process?"*

This questioning worksheet will help you structure your conversations effectively and gather the information needed to offer the right solution.

Listening Skills and Note-Taking

While asking the right questions is crucial, equally important is how well you listen to the responses. Active listening builds rapport, uncovers additional details, and helps you identify deeper needs. Listening isn't just about hearing; it's about making the other person feel understood.

Developing Active Listening Skills

To become an effective listener, follow these steps:

- ✓ Pay Full Attention: During conversations, avoid distractions. Put away your phone and focus solely on the speaker.

  Example: During a virtual meeting, minimize other open tabs to prevent distractions.
- ✓ Listen Without Interrupting: Let your prospect finish speaking before responding. Interrupting can make the other person feel rushed or undervalued.

  Example: If a customer is explaining their problem, resist the urge to jump in with a solution. Instead, nod to show you're engaged, but allow them to finish.
- ✓ Paraphrase What You've Heard: To ensure you've understood correctly, restate what the prospect has said in your own words.

  Example: "So, if I'm understanding correctly, your main concern is the inability to track shipments in real time, which is leading to delays in customer orders?"
- ✓ Ask Follow-Up Questions: Active listening involves digging deeper. After paraphrasing, ask follow-up questions to gain a more detailed understanding.

Example: "Can you tell me more about how these delays are impacting your customer satisfaction metrics?"

Listening Exercise

In your next meeting, set the goal to practice active listening using these steps:

- ✓ Before the meeting: Plan to actively listen by setting aside all distractions.
- ✓ During the meeting: Use techniques like paraphrasing and asking follow-up questions to confirm your understanding.
- ✓ After the meeting: Reflect on your performance. Did you fully focus on the conversation? Were you able to restate the customer's needs accurately? Identify any areas where you can improve your listening skills.

Proving Value with F.A.B. Selling

Once you have gathered all the necessary information, it's time to prove the value of your product or service. The F.A.B. (Features, Advantages, Benefits) framework is an excellent tool to help you demonstrate how your offering meets the prospect's needs. This framework enables you to go beyond listing features and connect those features to real, tangible benefits for the customer.

Understanding the F.A.B. Framework

- ✓ Features: These are the specific characteristics or functions of your product or service.

  Example: "Our project management tool includes automated task tracking."
- ✓ Advantages: Explain how these features help the prospect solve their problems.

Example: "With automated task tracking, your team won't need to spend time manually updating task lists."

- ✓ Benefits: Connect the advantages to the customer's specific needs, explaining how they will gain value.

  Example: "This means your team can focus on more critical tasks, increasing productivity and helping you meet deadlines faster."

By framing the conversation around the F.A.B. structure, you demonstrate how your product or service provides real value to the customer.

Exercise: FAB Worksheet

To practice using the F.A.B. framework, complete the following steps:

- ✓ Step 1: Select one of your top-selling products or services and list its key features.

  Example: Your company sells a customer relationship management (CRM) software.

  Feature: "*Our CRM system integrates with popular email platforms.*"
- ✓ Step 2: Identify how each feature provides an advantage to the customer.

  Advantage: *"By integrating with email platforms, you can streamline communication and ensure that every customer interaction is captured."*
- ✓ Step 3: Write out the specific benefits that this advantage brings to the customer.

  Benefit: *"This means your sales team will never miss important customer emails, leading to better follow-ups, increased customer satisfaction, and ultimately more sales."*

Uncovering needs and building value are fundamental aspects of successful selling. By mastering the art of asking effective questions, listening actively, and using the F.A.B. framework, you'll be able to build stronger connections with your prospects and prove that your product or service is the right solution to their problems.

Through the exercises provided, you can implement these techniques step by step and practice in real-life situations. With time and practice, these skills will become second nature, enabling you to uncover needs more effectively and demonstrate value in every sales conversation.

Handling Objections Effectively

In sales, objections are inevitable. No matter how well-prepared you are or how much value you provide, potential customers will often raise concerns or doubts. However, objections are not always negative—they are opportunities to engage further, uncover deeper needs, and build stronger relationships. When you handle objections effectively, you demonstrate your understanding of the customer's situation and show that you have their best interests at heart.

This chapter will equip you with practical strategies to understand why customers object, address their concerns, and turn objections into opportunities. By mastering these techniques, you'll become more confident in your sales conversations and more effective at closing deals.

Understanding Why Customers Object

Objections are not necessarily a sign that the customer is uninterested. More often than not, objections arise because customers have unresolved concerns, incomplete information, or fear about making a wrong decision. To handle objections effectively, it's crucial to understand the underlying reasons behind them.

Some common reasons for objections include:

- ✓ Lack of Understanding: The customer may not fully understand the value of your product or how it solves their problem.
- ✓ Perceived Risk: They may have concerns about the risks involved, such as whether the

product will work as promised, or if it's worth the investment.

- ✓ Misalignment: The customer may feel that the product or service does not align with their current needs or priorities.
- ✓ Financial Constraints: Budget limitations or concerns about the price can lead to objections, especially if they are unsure of the return on investment.

Analyzing Common Reasons Behind Objections

To better prepare for objections, it's essential to analyze the reasons behind them. Think about past conversations and consider what the most frequent objections were. Did customers express concerns about price, timing, or the product's effectiveness? Analyzing the patterns behind objections will help you anticipate them in future sales conversations.

Exercise: Objections Log Template

To keep track of objections and improve your responses, use an Objections Log. This log will allow you to record the objections you encounter, analyze their root causes, and develop potential responses.

Here's how to use the Objections Log:

- ✓ Step 1: After each sales conversation, record any objections the customer raised.
  Example: *"The product is too expensive,"* or *"We don't need this right now."*
- ✓ Step 2: Analyze the root cause of the objection. Was it a financial concern, a lack of understanding, or a perceived misalignment?
  Example: If the customer says, *"It's too expensive,"* the root cause could be that they don't yet see the value in the product relative to its price.

- ✓ Step 3: Develop potential responses for each objection. These responses should address the customer's underlying concerns.
  Example: *"I understand that the price is a concern. Can I show you how this solution can save your team time and money over the long term?"*
- ✓ Step 4: Review your log regularly to refine your responses and identify any recurring objections.

By using an Objections Log, you'll gain a deeper understanding of customer concerns and improve your ability to address them effectively.

The Objection-Handling Process

Handling objections effectively requires a structured approach. Rather than reacting defensively, a well-thought-out process can help you manage objections calmly and confidently. Below is a step-by-step guide for addressing and overcoming objections.

Step-by-Step Guide for Addressing Objections

- ✓ Acknowledge the Objection: The first step in handling any objection is to acknowledge it. Show empathy and understanding to ensure the customer feels heard.
  Example: If a customer says, *"This product seems too expensive for us right now," respond with, "I completely understand your concern about the price."*
- ✓ Clarify and Explore: Before responding, clarify the objection to ensure you understand the root issue. Ask follow-up questions to explore the customer's concerns further.
  Example: "*When you say the price seems high, do you mean in comparison to your*

budget, or is it that you're not sure about the value it provides?"

- ✓ Validate the Concern: Show the customer that their objection is valid. This will help build trust and rapport.
  Example*: "I can see why you'd feel that way, especially if you've had experiences where the return didn't justify the investment."*
- ✓ Provide a Response: Now that you've clarified and validated the objection, provide a thoughtful response that addresses their concern. Use data, testimonials, or other supporting evidence to back up your response.
  Example: *"One thing I'd like to point out is that while the upfront cost may seem high, our clients often find that the savings they achieve from increased productivity more than covers the cost within six months."*
- ✓ Confirm and Close: Once you've addressed the objection, confirm with the customer to ensure their concern has been resolved. Then, guide the conversation toward the next steps.
  Example: *"Does that help clarify the pricing structure? If you're comfortable moving forward, I can walk you through the next steps."*

Exercise: Objection-Handling Worksheet

To practice handling objections, complete the following steps:

- ✓ Step 1: Write down three common objections you face in your sales conversations.

Example: *"The product is too expensive," "We don't need this right now," "I'm not sure if this will work for us."*

- ✓ Step 2: For each objection, apply the five-step process.

- Acknowledge the objection: "I understand your concern."
- Clarify: *"Is your concern about the budget, or are you unsure about the return on investment?"*
- Validate: *"That's a completely valid concern, especially in the current financial climate."*
- Respond: "*Let me show you how this solution can actually save your company money in the long term."*
- Confirm: *"Does that address your concern? Should we proceed with the next steps?"*

By practicing with this worksheet, you'll become more confident in handling objections during your sales conversations.

Common Key Objections:

NO MONEY, NO HURRY, NO CONFIDENCE, NO NEED

Throughout your sales career, you'll encounter a range of objections. However, most objections can be categorized into four key types: No Money, No Hurry, No Confidence, and No Need. Let's explore each in detail and learn how to address them effectively.

No Money

This is one of the most common objections: *"We don't have the budget,"* or *"It's too expensive."* To handle the No Money objection, you need to demonstrate the long-term value of your solution.

Show how the product can save money, increase revenue, or provide a return on investment.

Example:

Customer: "*We can't afford this product right now.*"

Response: *"I understand. Many of our clients had similar concerns at first. However, they've found that the cost is quickly offset by the savings in time and increased efficiency. Would it be helpful if I walked you through the potential savings this could offer?"*

No Hurry

The No Hurry objection arises when customers don't see the urgency in making a decision. They may say, *"We don't need this right now,"* or *"We'll think about it later."* To address this objection, create urgency by highlighting the risks of delaying the decision or showing how immediate action can lead to faster results.

Example:

Customer: *"We'll look into this next quarter."*

Response: *"I understand the desire to take your time. However, by implementing this solution now, you'll start seeing results in the next few months, which could give you a competitive edge. Waiting could cost more in the long run."*

No Confidence

When customers express the No Confidence objection, they may be unsure whether the product will deliver on its promises. They could say, "*I'm not sure this will work for us,*" or *"We've tried similar solutions before."* To overcome this, provide proof in the form of case studies, testimonials, or a money-back guarantee to reassure them.

Example:

Customer: *"I'm not sure if this will work for us."*

Response: *"I understand your hesitation. Let me share some examples of companies similar to yours that have successfully implemented our solution. I'm confident that you'll see the same kind of results."*

No Need

The No Need objection is when the customer doesn't perceive a strong enough need for your product. They might say, *"We don't need this,"* or *"We're doing fine without it."* In this case, your goal is to uncover deeper needs that the customer might not have considered and demonstrate how your solution addresses those needs.

Example:

Customer: *"We don't really need this product."*

Response: *"I hear you. From our previous conversations, though, I remember you mentioned that keeping track of customer data was a challenge. Our solution can help you streamline that process, saving you time and preventing errors. Could that be helpful?"*

Handling the PRICE Objection

Price is one of the most common objections, and handling it well can make the difference between closing or losing a sale. When addressing the price objection, it's important to focus on the value your product brings rather than the cost alone.

Here's a step-by-step approach to handling the price objection:

1. Acknowledge the Concern: Start by showing understanding and empathy.

   Example: "I completely understand that the price might seem high at first glance."
2. Ask Questions to Clarify: Find out if the customer's concern is about the overall cost or

if they need more clarity on the value they'll receive.
Example: "Is your concern primarily with the budget, or would it help to see how this investment can generate returns for your business?"

3. Refocus on Value: Shift the conversation from price to value. Emphasize the benefits your solution offers and how it can provide a return on investment.
Example: "While the upfront cost may seem significant, the long-term savings and increased efficiency more than make up for it. Let me show you how our other clients have experienced a positive ROI within the first year."
4. Provide Alternatives: If budget constraints are genuine, offer alternative payment plans, discounts, or scaled-back versions of your product to accommodate their needs.
Example: "We also offer flexible payment options or a scaled version of the solution that fits within your current budget."
5. Reiterate Results and Close: After addressing the price concern, steer the conversation toward the next steps.
Example: "Does that help clarify the pricing? If so, we can proceed with the paperwork and get started on implementation."

In conclusion, objections are not roadblocks—they are opportunities to provide more information, address concerns, and build stronger relationships with your customers. By mastering the objection-handling process and understanding the key objections you'll face, you can turn objections into opportunities to close more deals.

Negotiation Skills

Negotiation is one of the most critical skills in any business transaction, and mastering it can make all the difference between a deal that adds value and one that leaves money on the table. Negotiation is not just about haggling over prices; it is the art of creating a win-win situation where both parties feel satisfied. When approached with preparation, understanding, and empathy, negotiation becomes an opportunity to build long-term partnerships that benefit everyone involved.

In this chapter, we will dive deep into the essentials of negotiation—what it is, why it matters, the steps to follow, and how to refine this skill through practice. By the end of this chapter, you will have a structured approach to negotiation, allowing you to maximize the value you bring to the table while fostering positive relationships.

What is Negotiation and Why It's Important

Negotiation is a process in which two or more parties work together to reach a mutually acceptable agreement. It involves communication, compromise, and strategy. Whether you're negotiating a contract, salary, deal terms, or even small details of a project, negotiation helps you achieve your objectives while ensuring that the other party's needs are met as well. The ultimate goal is to create a situation where both parties walk away feeling satisfied.

Understanding the Basics of Negotiation

At its core, negotiation is about finding common ground and resolving differences. It's not about "winning" or "losing"—successful negotiation means both parties get something they value. Understanding this can shift your mindset from one of competition to one of collaboration.

The key components of a successful negotiation include:

- ✓ Preparation: Knowing what you want and what you're willing to concede is essential. Walking into a negotiation unprepared often leads to poor outcomes.
- ✓ Active Listening: Listening carefully to the other party's needs, concerns, and objectives is crucial to finding solutions that work for both sides.
- ✓ Clear Communication: Articulating your points clearly and without aggression ensures that both parties remain on the same page throughout the negotiation process.
- ✓ Problem-Solving Attitude: A negotiation should be seen as a problem-solving exercise rather than a confrontation. Focus on how both parties can leave with value.
- ✓ Flexibility: Successful negotiators are flexible. While you should have a clear idea of your goals, it's essential to adapt to new information and changing circumstances.

Exercise: Negotiation Objective Worksheet

Before entering any negotiation, it is important to clearly define what you want to achieve. This can be done through a Negotiation Objective Worksheet, which will help you outline your goals, understand your non-negotiables, and consider potential trade-offs.

Step-by-step guide for filling out the Negotiation Objective Worksheet:

- ✓ Step 1: Write down your primary goal for the negotiation. Be specific and measurable.
  Example: If you are negotiating a sales contract, your primary goal might be to close a deal worth $50,000 within the next three months.
- ✓ Step 2: List your secondary goals. These are additional objectives that would be desirable but not essential.
  Example: As a secondary goal, you might want to negotiate for a faster payment schedule or get an agreement on future repeat business.
- ✓ Step 3: Define your "walk-away" point. This is the point beyond which the deal is no longer worth it for you. Knowing this ahead of time prevents you from making poor decisions under pressure.
  Example: Your walk-away point could be that you will not accept anything less than $45,000 for the deal.
- ✓ Step 4: Identify potential trade-offs. Think about areas where you can afford to be flexible or concede something to the other party.
  Example: You might be willing to offer a longer warranty period if the client agrees to the price you are asking.
- ✓ Step 5: Consider the other party's perspective. What do they likely want out of this negotiation? Understanding their objectives will help you find areas for mutual benefit.

Example: The client might be most concerned about minimizing upfront costs. You could offer a payment plan to meet their needs.

By filling out this worksheet before every negotiation, you will go into the conversation with a clear sense of purpose, ensuring that you stay focused on your objectives while remaining open to compromise where necessary.

The 5 Steps of Negotiation

Successful negotiation follows a structured process. While each negotiation is different, following these five steps will help you approach negotiations with confidence and maximize your chances of reaching a satisfactory agreement.

- ✓ Step 1: Preparation
- Preparation is the foundation of any successful negotiation. Before you enter into any discussion, research the situation thoroughly. Know your objectives, understand the market conditions, and gather as much information as possible about the other party.
  Example: If you're negotiating with a supplier, make sure you understand the cost of goods, industry standards, and the supplier's position in the market. This knowledge will give you leverage and allow you to make informed decisions.
- Key preparation tasks:
  Identify your goals and your walk-away point.
  Research the other party's needs, priorities, and possible constraints.
  Gather relevant data or evidence to support your position.
- ✓ Step 2: Opening the Discussion

The opening phase of the negotiation sets the tone for the entire conversation. Begin by stating your objectives clearly but in a non-confrontational way. Establish rapport and make the other party feel comfortable.

Example: If you're negotiating a contract, you might say, *"I'm looking forward to finding a solution that works for both of us. My goal is to secure a deal that meets our budget while ensuring timely delivery on your end."*

It's important to establish a positive and cooperative atmosphere at the outset. This helps build trust and encourages the other party to approach the conversation with a collaborative mindset.

✓ Step 3: Understanding the Other Party's Position

Listening is a critical skill in negotiation. Once the discussion has started, focus on understanding the other party's needs and concerns. Ask open-ended questions to encourage them to share more information.

Example: Ask questions like, *"What are your main priorities for this project?" or "What concerns do you have about the timeline?"*

By understanding their position, you'll be better equipped to propose solutions that address their concerns while still meeting your objectives. Active listening also shows that you are invested in reaching a fair agreement.

✓ Step 4: Proposing Solutions

After both parties have shared their positions, it's time to propose potential solutions. Frame your suggestions in a way that shows how they can benefit both sides. Be creative—

sometimes the best solutions are not the most obvious.

Example: "If we can extend the contract by six months, I can offer you a discount on the overall project cost. This would give us more time to ensure the highest quality work, while also saving you money."

Be prepared to make trade-offs, but always keep your core objectives in mind. Focus on achieving the most value for both parties.

- ✓ Step 5: Closing the Deal

The final stage of the negotiation is reaching an agreement. Once both parties have come to a consensus, confirm the terms and clarify any outstanding points. Make sure there is mutual understanding before moving forward.

Example: Summarize the agreement: "So we've agreed on a $50,000 contract, with a delivery timeline of 90 days, and a payment schedule of 30% upfront and the remaining 70% upon completion. Does that sound correct?"

After confirming the agreement, take steps to formalize it, such as drafting a contract or getting verbal commitments. Ensure that both parties leave the negotiation feeling satisfied and clear on the next steps.

Exercise: Negotiation Role-Play

One of the best ways to improve your negotiation skills is through practice. Role-playing different negotiation scenarios with a partner allows you to test different strategies, experiment with responses, and build confidence in a low-risk environment.

Here's how to conduct a negotiation role-play exercise:

- ✓ Step 1: Choose a real-life negotiation scenario. This could be a past negotiation or an upcoming one that you want to prepare for. Example: You are negotiating a service contract with a client who is asking for a 15% discount.
- ✓ Step 2: Assign roles. One person will play the role of the negotiator (you), and the other will play the role of the client or counterpart. Example: The client might start by saying, *"I like your proposal, but I can't justify the price. I'll need a 15% discount if we're going to move forward."*
- ✓ Step 3: Begin the negotiation. The negotiator should use the five steps outlined in this chapter: preparation, opening the discussion, understanding the other party's position, proposing solutions, and closing the deal. Example: The negotiator might respond, *"I understand your budget constraints. However, we can't offer a 15% discount. What I can do is offer a smaller discount if we extend the contract for additional services."*
- ✓ Step 4: Reflect on the exercise. After the role-play is complete, discuss how the negotiation went. What strategies worked well? Where did you encounter challenges? How could you improve in future negotiations?
- ✓ Step 5: Repeat the exercise with different scenarios. The more you practice, the more confident and prepared you'll feel when it's time to negotiate in real life.

Final Thoughts on Negotiation Skills

Negotiation is not just a transactional skill—it’s a relationship-building one. By approaching negotiations with empathy, preparation, and flexibility, you can create win-win outcomes that maximize value for both parties. Whether you're negotiating multi-million-dollar contracts or day-to-day agreements, these skills will set you apart as a professional who can achieve results while fostering positive, long-term relationships. With practice and a clear strategy, you will become more adept at navigating the nuances of negotiation and securing outcomes that benefit all involved.

Enhancing Sales through Up-Selling and Cross-Selling

One of the most effective ways to maximize revenue and improve customer satisfaction is through up-selling and cross-selling. These strategic selling techniques go beyond the initial sale, helping sales professionals deepen their relationship with customers while providing additional value. The goal is not to push unnecessary products or services, but to identify the customer's needs and offer solutions that improve their overall experience.

In this chapter, we will explore the concepts of up-selling and cross-selling in detail, how to recognize and leverage opportunities, and how to implement these strategies without being overbearing. By the end, you'll have a thorough understanding of how to increase revenue while building stronger relationships with clients through these techniques.

Up-Selling and Cross-Selling Defined

Up-selling is the practice of encouraging customers to purchase a more expensive or upgraded version of a product or service they are already interested in. This could involve adding extra features, upgrading to a premium model, or extending a service package. The key to up-selling is to highlight the additional value the customer will gain by investing more. It's not about pushing the most expensive option, but rather about finding a solution that enhances the customer's experience or results.

Cross-selling, on the other hand, involves offering complementary products or services that enhance or complement the original purchase. Cross-selling is about showing the customer how different products or services can work together to meet their broader needs. For example, if a customer is buying a computer, cross-selling might involve suggesting software, accessories, or a maintenance plan that complements the initial purchase.

The success of both up-selling and cross-selling relies on trust and relevance. The customer needs to believe that you have their best interests in mind, and the recommendations should make sense based on what they truly need. If done well, these strategies not only increase sales but also improve customer satisfaction by providing a more complete solution to their problems.

Identifying Opportunities for Up-Selling and Cross-Selling

Recognizing the right moment to offer an up-sell or cross-sell is key to success. Timing and relevance are everything. The first step in identifying these opportunities is understanding the customer's needs in detail. If you know why they are purchasing a particular product or service, you can better determine what additional value might be meaningful to them.

How to Identify Up-Selling Opportunities

- ✓ Understanding the Customer's Goals: Always keep in mind the customer's objectives and desired outcomes. If a client is looking to solve a problem or achieve a specific goal, up-selling to a premium product or additional service makes sense when it genuinely enhances their ability to achieve that goal.

  Example: A customer looking for a laptop for professional video editing may initially choose a basic model. However, if you know that they will need high processing power, extra storage, and a better graphics card for efficient work, you can offer an upgraded model. The conversation could go like this: *"The model you've chosen is good for general use, but since you're working with video editing software, you might want to consider upgrading to this model. It has faster processing, more RAM, and a high-performance graphics card. This will make editing videos much smoother and save you time in the long run."*

- ✓ Leverage Data: If you have access to previous purchasing data or usage habits, this information can provide insight into which products or services may be most beneficial for a customer. If a customer is consistently using a product at its maximum capacity, you can recommend an upgraded version that offers more features or greater efficiency.
  Example: If a customer is using a basic cloud storage plan and is consistently reaching the storage limit, you can suggest upgrading to a larger storage package: *"I noticed you're close to hitting your storage limit. We have a plan that offers twice the space, and it includes additional backup features to keep your files secure."*

How to Identify Cross-Selling Opportunities

- ✓ Complementary Products or Services: When cross-selling, you are essentially bundling products or services that make sense together. Think about what additional products or services could enhance the customer's experience or the value they get from their initial purchase.

Example: A customer purchasing a smartphone might benefit from accessories like a protective case, screen guard, or wireless charger. In this case, you might say, *"To protect your phone, you might also want to consider this durable case. It's custom-fit for your model and will help keep it safe from drops and scratches."*

- ✓ Long-Term Needs: Consider the customer's long-term use of the product or service and how other offerings could make their life easier in the future. This works especially well when dealing with products or services that have ongoing maintenance or consumable needs.

  Example: If a client buys a printer, you can cross-sell ink cartridges or paper: *"You'll need these cartridges for your printer, and we have a package deal that gives you 20% off if you buy them together with the printer today."*

Practical Examples of Up-Selling and Cross-Selling

To see these techniques in action, let's look at some specific examples across different industries:

Retail Electronics:

- ✓ Up-selling: A customer buying a standard laptop for work could be offered a higher-end model with more processing power, better battery life, or additional storage if they plan to use it for more demanding tasks.
- ✓ Cross-selling: The same customer could be offered a laptop bag, external mouse, or an

extended warranty as complementary purchases.

Hospitality:

- ✓ Up-selling: A guest booking a standard hotel room could be offered a suite with a better view, extra amenities like a jacuzzi, or access to the executive lounge for a small additional fee.
- ✓ Cross-selling: The guest could be offered complementary services such as spa treatments, guided tours, or dining vouchers.

Software Sales:

- ✓ Up-selling: A business purchasing a basic software package could be offered a premium version that includes additional features like advanced reporting, customization options, or faster customer support.
- ✓ Cross-selling: The business could also be offered related services such as training for their employees or a service plan for future software updates.

These examples demonstrate that up-selling and cross-selling are not about pushing unnecessary products but about adding value to the customer's experience. When done right, these strategies help the customer see how investing in more or complementary options can meet their needs better.

Exercise: Up-Selling and Cross-Selling Practice

This exercise will help you practice identifying opportunities for up-selling and cross-selling with real clients or hypothetical scenarios. You will follow a step-by-step process to develop a personalized approach to each situation.

- ✓ Step 1: Select a product or service that you frequently sell. This could be anything from electronics, software, to professional services.
  Example: A car dealership selling mid-range family sedans.
- ✓ Step 2: Identify an up-selling opportunity. Think about what higher-value options are available within the same product or service category that would genuinely benefit the customer based on their needs.
  Example: You notice that a customer who is looking at a mid-range sedan will benefit more from the top-tier model because it has better safety features, enhanced fuel efficiency, and a more advanced entertainment system.
- ✓ Step 3: Develop your pitch. Craft a conversation that focuses on the additional value the customer will get from the upgraded option.
  Example: "I see you're interested in the mid-range sedan, which is a great choice for families. However, for just a little extra, you can get the upgraded model with enhanced safety features like lane departure warnings and a better fuel economy that will save you money in the long run."
- ✓ Step 4: Identify a cross-selling opportunity. Consider what products or services would complement the initial purchase and provide the customer with a better overall experience.
  Example: For the same customer, you could offer complementary services like an extended warranty or roadside assistance. You might say, "We also have an extended warranty package that covers all repairs for five years,

which would give you peace of mind and save on future maintenance costs."

- ✓ Step 5: Role-play the interaction. Practice your up-sell and cross-sell pitches with a colleague or friend, focusing on how to naturally weave them into the conversation without sounding pushy.
- ✓ Step 6: Reflect on the role-play. After practicing, think about what went well and where you can improve. Did the up-sell or cross-sell feel natural? Did you provide enough value to make it worth the customer's consideration?
- ✓ Step 7: Apply it with real clients. Take what you've learned from the exercise and start applying it in your actual sales interactions. Pay attention to how customers respond to your suggestions and adjust your approach based on their feedback.

Final Thoughts on Up-Selling and Cross-Selling

Up-selling and cross-selling are powerful tools that can significantly boost revenue and enhance customer relationships when used strategically. By focusing on the customer's needs and offering genuine value, these techniques can help customers feel more satisfied with their purchases while helping you achieve your sales targets. Remember, the key is to always approach these conversations with the customer's best interests at heart, ensuring that every recommendation you make is relevant and beneficial to them. With practice and careful application, you will master the art of up-selling and cross-selling, leading to greater success in your sales career.

Delivering Exceptional Customer Service

The key to a successful, sustainable sales career is not just acquiring new customers but retaining them. Exceptional customer service is the foundation of long-lasting relationships with clients, and it can significantly enhance your sales outcomes over time. A client who is satisfied with both the product and the experience of purchasing it is more likely to return, provide referrals, and give positive reviews, which are all essential for growing your business. In this chapter, we will delve deeply into what it means to deliver exceptional customer service, the role it plays in customer retention, and how to implement strategies that ensure clients stay loyal over time.

The Two Cs to Worry About: The Customer in Front and the Competition Behind

Sales professionals often focus too much on acquiring new customers without realizing that retaining existing customers can be just as important—if not more so. The two key forces that must always be in your mind are the *customer in front* and the *competition behind*. The customer in front represents the clients you currently have, while the competition behind refers to your competitors who are constantly trying to win over your customers.

The Customer in Front

Maintaining strong, lasting relationships with your current clients is the first priority. This is where exceptional customer service comes into play. You can't afford to only provide great service during the initial sale; it must continue well after the transaction is complete. Customers want to feel valued beyond the moment they hand over their money. How you treat them after the sale plays a major role in their decision to come back and make repeat purchases.

Building trust, being available for assistance, and providing value after the initial transaction is critical to establishing this relationship. Always remember that your existing customers are your best salespeople; if they are satisfied, they will not only continue to purchase from you but also recommend your services to others.

The Competition Behind

Never forget that your competitors are always looking for an opportunity to steal your customers. They may offer better prices, faster delivery, or seemingly superior customer service. The best way to fend off this competition is by providing unparalleled customer service that makes it difficult for customers to even consider going elsewhere. A satisfied customer is much less likely to switch to a competitor, even if they are presented with a cheaper or seemingly more convenient option.

Here is an example: Imagine you have a loyal customer who purchases your software product. They are satisfied with the functionality, but they've heard about a competitor offering a similar product at a lower price. If you've established a strong relationship and regularly check in with them to offer support, updates, and additional services, the likelihood of them switching will decrease. Even if the competitor offers a discount, the value you've provided through consistent and exceptional service can outweigh the monetary savings.

Maintaining Relationships After the Sale

The key to exceptional customer service is maintaining relationships after the sale is complete. This requires ongoing communication and follow-up, but it must be done in a way that feels genuine and not just another sales tactic. Your goal is to continue adding value, ensuring the customer remains satisfied with their purchase, and being there to resolve any potential issues before they become bigger problems.

Example of Ongoing Relationship Management:

Let's say you sell office equipment to a client. After the sale, it's not enough to assume the deal is over. Instead, you might follow up with a call a week after delivery to ask how the equipment is working and if they have any questions. You could also schedule periodic check-ins every six months to make sure everything is functioning well and to see if they have additional needs that you can help with.

Exercise 1: Customer Follow-Up Template

To help ensure consistent follow-up with clients, it's useful to establish a follow-up schedule. A well-planned schedule makes sure that your clients are never forgotten or ignored and that their needs are always being addressed.

Step 1: Start by creating a follow-up schedule for all clients. It's important to have specific touchpoints over time, such as after the sale, a few months later, and around product renewal times.

Example Template:

- ✓ Day 1 (After Purchase): Send a personalized thank you note or email expressing gratitude for their purchase.

Example: *"Thank you for choosing our services! We're excited to work with you, and I'm here to assist you with anything you need."*

- ✓ Day 7: A week after the purchase, call the client to ask how everything is going and whether they have any questions or concerns.
  Example: *"Hi [Client's Name], it's been about a week since you received your [product/service], and I wanted to check in to see how things are going. Is there anything I can assist you with?"*
- ✓ Month 1: A month later, send a follow-up message or call to see if they are fully satisfied and to inquire about any feedback or suggestions.
  Example: *"Hi [Client's Name], just checking in to see if you're still satisfied with everything. Your feedback is very important to us!"*
- ✓ Month 6: Every six months, send an email or make a call to offer support and ensure the client is getting the most value out of the product.
  Example: *"Hi [Client's Name], it's been a few months now, and I'd love to hear how [product/service] is working for you. Is there anything I can help you with to ensure you're getting the most out of it?"*
- ✓ Annual Check-In: Once a year, check in for long-term customers to ensure their satisfaction and to remind them of any updates or new offerings you have that could benefit them.

Step 2: Record each interaction in a customer relationship management (CRM) system or a simple spreadsheet, noting the date, key points discussed, and any follow-up actions needed.

Example:

Date	Customer Name	Interaction Type	Key Points Discussed	Follow-Up Action
01/01/2024	John Doe	Purchase Follow-Up	Product received, no issues so far	Check again in 1 week
01/08/2024	John Doe	Phone Call	Customer satisfied, asked about upgrades	Send upgrade details

By using a template like this, you can ensure that no customer is forgotten, and every relationship is nurtured over time.

The Lifetime Value of a Customer

The lifetime value (LTV) of a customer refers to the total revenue you can expect from that customer over the entirety of your relationship with them. It's crucial to understand that a single sale is not the end of your engagement with a client, and focusing on long-term relationships can provide significant returns.

For example, let's assume a customer purchases an item from you for $1,000. If you only focus on that single transaction, you might think the value of the customer is $1,000. But if you provide exceptional service and maintain that relationship over several years, they could make multiple purchases, upgrade their products, or refer new clients to you. In the long run, the total value of that customer could be far greater—potentially tens of thousands of dollars.

Understanding the lifetime value of a customer shifts your mindset. You'll begin to see customers as ongoing partners rather than one-time transactions, making it easier to invest time and effort in ensuring they remain loyal to your business.

Exercise 2: Customer Retention Plan

Creating a customer retention plan is essential for ensuring that your clients remain engaged with your business over the long term. This exercise will walk you through how to create a retention plan, ensuring you have strategies in place to foster loyalty and maximize the lifetime value of each customer.

- ✓ Step 1: Understand your customer's needs. Before you can create a customer retention plan, you need to fully understand what your customers want and expect. Conduct surveys or simply ask them during your follow-up calls what challenges they're facing, what they enjoy about your product, and where you can improve. This feedback will be invaluable in shaping your retention efforts.
- ✓ Step 2: Build a communication strategy. Decide how and when you will stay in touch with your customers. Will you send regular emails, make phone calls, or set up meetings? Communication should be consistent but not overwhelming. Set up reminders to reach out at important touchpoints, such as after product purchases, renewals, or when new features or products are available.
- ✓ Step 3: Offer incentives for loyalty. Consider ways to reward long-term customers for their loyalty. This could include discounts, special offers, or even exclusive products or services

only available to long-term clients. The key is to make them feel appreciated for sticking with you.

- ✓ Step 4: Provide exceptional post-sale support. One of the best ways to retain customers is by offering outstanding support after the sale. Ensure that customers have easy access to help, whether through a dedicated customer service line, online chat, or an account manager. Resolve issues quickly, and always follow up to ensure that the problem has been fully resolved.
- ✓ Step 5: Measure your retention efforts. To ensure your customer retention strategies are working, you need to track key metrics, such as repeat purchase rates, customer satisfaction scores, and churn rates (the percentage of customers who leave). Use this data to continually improve your approach.

Example of a Retention Strategy: Let's say you're running an online subscription service for software tools. A good customer retention strategy could involve sending out regular newsletters with tips and tricks on how to get the most out of the software, offering special discounts to long-term subscribers, and hosting exclusive webinars where customers can learn advanced features.

Over time, you would track the number of renewals and customer satisfaction surveys to see if these efforts are improving retention. If you notice churn rates are high after the first year, you might increase your communication and offer a special deal before their subscription expires.

Delivering exceptional customer service requires commitment, empathy, and consistency. By focusing on the needs of the customer in front and understanding the competition behind, you can secure lasting relationships and prevent your clients from looking elsewhere. Building a comprehensive follow-up system, understanding the lifetime value of each customer, and implementing a retention plan will not only foster customer loyalty but will also set your business apart in the long term.

Remember, customer service doesn't stop after the sale—it's an ongoing process that ensures your customers are happy, engaged, and loyal for life. By taking the steps laid out in this chapter and making customer service a central part of your strategy, you'll build a strong foundation for success in the competitive world of sales.

Call Evaluation Format

This format evaluates your Sales Performance during or after a sales call or role-play based on preparation, the approach, discovery of client needs, proving value, and closing, while emphasizing professionalism throughout the interaction.

Name of Salesperson: ______________________
Client: ____________________________________
Evaluator: _______________ **Date of Call:** _______

EVALUATION CATEGORIES

Steps	Good	Average	Poor	What I observed/Heard (Comments)
Preparation				
- Self-Motivation/Mental Readiness				
- Understanding Client Background				
- Market and Competitor Knowledge				
- Clear Sales Strategy (Goals/ Questions)				
Introduction & Approach				
- Greeting and Introduction				
- Building Initial Rapport				
- Setting the Call Agenda				
Fact-Finding/Discovery				
- Uncovering Client's Pain Points/ Needs				
- Asking Open-Ended Questions				
- Active Listening				
- Summarizing Client's Problems				

Proving Value & Solutions				
- Presenting Unique Value Proposition (USP)				
- Demonstrating Product Benefits (FAB)				
- Handling Objections Professionally				
- Providing Relevant Solutions				

Closing				
- Summarizing Agreement				
- Gaining Commitment (Next Steps)				
- Thanking the Client				
Professional Conduct				
- Tone of Voice and Confidence				
- Use of Professional Language				
- Grooming and Overall Demeanor				

General Feedback:

Action Points for Improvement:

Evaluator's Signature: ______________________________
Salesperson's Signature: ___________________________

Master Action Plan: Embedding Sales Skills into Your Daily Routine

In this final chapter, we'll focus on building a *Master Action Plan* that will help you practice and embed the key skills from this book into your daily sales routine. This plan is designed to help you turn these skills into habits so that they become part of your selling system.

Step 1: Daily Preparation Routine

Before you begin your day, it's crucial to prepare both mentally and strategically for the calls or meetings ahead. Preparation builds confidence and ensures you're ready for any situation.

- ✓ Self-Motivation:
  Action: Begin each day by revisiting your personal and professional goals. Visualize a successful day.
  Example: Before your calls, take five minutes to mentally rehearse a positive client conversation. This helps reduce anxiety and primes you for success.
- ✓ Know Your Client:
  Action: Review the profiles of the clients you will be engaging with that day.
  Example: If you are speaking with a manufacturing company, familiarize yourself with their latest product releases or industry trends. Note down three specific client details you will bring up on the call to build rapport.
- ✓ Prepare Your Tools:

Action: Make sure your CRM is updated, and your sales tools (brochures, scripts, presentations) are ready.
Example: If you have a demo scheduled, ensure that your slides or online product demos are pre-tested and available on all devices.

Step 2: Daily Role-Play Practice

Practicing role-plays helps build your sales skills and confidence in handling different situations. Set aside time every day to practice with a colleague or alone.

- ✓ 2.1 Set a Daily Role-Play Goal:
  Action: Dedicate at least 15-20 minutes to a role-play session every day.
  Example: Role-play an objection-handling scenario where a client questions the price of your product. Your goal is to overcome the objection using value-based selling techniques covered in this book.
- ✓ 2.2 Focus on One Skill at a Time:
  Action: Pick one area to focus on during your role-play (e.g., fact-finding, closing, handling objections).
  Example: Spend a day practicing active listening by asking open-ended questions and summarizing the client's responses.
- ✓ 2.3 Self-Evaluation and Feedback:
  Action: After each role-play, assess your performance using the Call Evaluation Format discussed earlier.
  Example: Record yourself during role-plays, and evaluate your performance based on how well you built rapport, presented solutions, and closed the conversation.

Step 3: Conduct Daily Sales Calls with Intent

Every sales call is an opportunity to sharpen your skills. Use each interaction to focus on a particular part of the sales process.

- ✓ 3.1 Set a Goal for Each Call:
  Action: Before each call, identify what success looks like (e.g., uncovering a new pain point, securing a follow-up meeting).
  Example: If your client has been hesitant to move forward, make your goal to identify their biggest hesitation and propose a solution by the end of the call.
- ✓ 3.2 Use Discovery Questions to Learn More:
  Action: Develop a list of probing, open-ended questions that you will use to uncover client needs.
  Example: "What challenges are you currently facing with your existing solution?" or "What goals are you hoping to achieve in the next quarter?"
- ✓ 3.3 Practice Active Listening:
  Action: During each call, practice active listening by summarizing the client's pain points and concerns.
  Example: "From what I understand, you're looking for a solution that saves you time without compromising on quality. Is that correct?"

Step 4: Weekly Reflection and Adjustment

Reflecting on your weekly performance allows you to track your progress and identify areas for improvement.

- ✓ 4.1 Review Your Week:

Action: At the end of each week, review the calls and meetings you've had, using the Call Evaluation Format to assess your performance.
Example: Identify patterns—are there objections you handle poorly? Are there certain types of clients where you excel? Document these trends for improvement.

- ✓ 4.2 Set Goals for the Upcoming Week:
  Action: Based on your review, set specific goals for the next week (e.g., improving closing techniques, better rapport-building).
  Example: If you struggled with gaining commitments, your goal might be to practice closing questions like, "What's stopping you from moving forward today?" in all calls next week.
- ✓ 4.3 Seek Feedback from Peers or Mentors:
  Action: Ask a mentor or peer to review one of your recorded calls and provide feedback.
  Example: They may point out that your tone sounds rushed when discussing price or that you could ask more discovery questions earlier in the conversation.

Step 5: Implementing a Continuous Learning System

Sales is an ever-evolving profession, so it's important to keep learning and adapting your approach.

- ✓ 5.1 Invest in Continuous Learning:
  Action: Dedicate time each month to improving your sales skills through books, courses, or podcasts.

Example: Take a course on advanced objection handling or read books on consultative selling.

- ✓ 5.2 Track Your Progress Over Time:
  Action: Keep a journal where you track the areas you're improving and where you still need work.
  Example: If you set a goal to improve closing rates, write down how many deals you've successfully closed each month and what changes in approach you used.
- ✓ 5.3 Practice Beyond Work:
  Action: Engage in real-world conversations that help improve your sales skills. This could be negotiating in everyday situations like making a purchase or leading discussions in group settings.
  Example: Practice persuasion skills by convincing friends to try new activities or restaurants using consultative techniques.

Step 6: Create a Personal Accountability System
Accountability ensures that you consistently practice and improve.

- ✓ 6.1 Track Daily and Weekly Metrics:
  Action: Create a simple tracking sheet to document key metrics, such as calls made, meetings booked, objections handled, and deals closed.
  Example: "I will make 15 outbound calls today, handle at least 3 objections, and close 1 deal by the end of the week."
- ✓ 6.2 Use a Personal Accountability Partner:
  Action: Partner with a colleague or peer to check in regularly on progress.

Example: Set weekly check-ins with your partner to review your performance and hold each other accountable for hitting your targets.

Master Action Plan Example
John's Weekly Master Action Plan:
Daily Routine:

- ✓ Morning review of top three clients for the day.
- ✓ Conduct one 20-minute role-play focused on handling price objections.
- ✓ Conduct 10 outbound calls with the goal of booking 2 follow-up meetings.

Call Goals:

- ✓ Call 1: Identify the client's long-term business goals.
- ✓ Call 2: Close for a product demo.

Weekly Reflection:

- ✓ By Friday, review all 10 calls and identify the top 2 where you missed closing opportunities.
- ✓ Adjust discovery questions for next week's calls.
- ✓ Learning and Development:
- ✓ Watch a webinar on "Handling Difficult Negotiations" over the weekend.
- ✓ Accountability:
- ✓ Meet with accountability partner on Monday morning to discuss last week's call evaluations and role-plays.

By following this Master Action Plan daily, weekly, and monthly, you'll not only practice the skills outlined in this book but also integrate them into your routine, making them second nature. Success in sales isn't about mastering one or two techniques—it's about consistent, intentional practice, reflection, and adjustment. Keep this plan as a guide, and you'll see your sales performance improve steadily.

Appendix:
Practical Worksheets and Templates

The following section contains worksheets and templates designed to help you apply the strategies and lessons outlined in the previous chapters. These tools are essential for translating theory into actionable steps and will allow you to keep track of your daily activities, prospecting efforts, customer interactions, and much more. Use these templates regularly to develop stronger sales habits, refine your strategies, and improve your overall performance.

---

1. Daily Activity Tracker

The Daily Activity Tracker is essential for monitoring your productivity and progress each day. This tool helps you stay accountable to your goals and ensures that you focus on activities that drive results.

How to Use the Daily Activity Tracker:

- ✓ Start each day by identifying the key tasks that must be completed. These can include prospecting, client follow-up, preparation for presentations, and handling objections.
- ✓ Throughout the day, log your actions and note whether you completed them, what the outcome was, and any follow-up tasks required.
- ✓ At the end of each day, review your completed tasks and assess your productivity. What worked well? What could be improved?

Example:

Suppose your primary goal for the day is to connect with three potential clients. You would list this task at the start of the day, track the calls or emails sent, and then record the outcome—whether it was a successful connection, no response, or a need for follow-up.

Daily Activity Tracker Template:

Date	Activity	Status (Complete/ In Progress)	Outcome	Next Steps
[Date]	Call Client A	Complete	Positive response, follow-up needed	Send proposal by [specific date]
[Date]	Email Lead B	In Progress	No response	Follow-up call on [specific date]
[Date]	Prepare presentation for C	Complete	Ready for meeting tomorrow	Review materials before presentation

---

2. Prospecting Planner

Prospecting is the lifeblood of sales, and staying organized in your outreach efforts is critical to success. The Prospecting Planner helps you create a structured approach to contacting new leads, following up, and tracking the results of each interaction.

How to Use the Prospecting Planner:

- ✓ List your prospects for the week.
- ✓ For each prospect, note the type of outreach you'll be using (email, call, LinkedIn message, etc.), the date of the outreach, and the desired outcome (e.g., to schedule a meeting, send a proposal).
- ✓ Track the status of each prospect (e.g., awaiting reply, scheduled meeting, not interested).

Example:
Imagine you're targeting five companies this week. You'll list each prospect, their contact details, the method of outreach (email or phone), and what you

Prospecting Planner Template:

Prospect Name	Contact Info	Outreach Method	Date	Desired Outcome	Status
Company A	[Email/ Phone]	Email	[Date]	Set up a meeting	Awaiting response
Company B	[Email/ Phone]	Phone Call	[Date]	Schedule demo	Scheduled demo for [date]
Company C	[Email/ Phone]	LinkedIn Message	[Date]	Send proposal	Sent proposal, awaiting reply

hope to achieve (such as scheduling a product demo).

---

3. Customer Profile Sheet
Understanding your customers in detail will allow you to tailor your approach and better meet their needs. The Customer Profile Sheet is a template for gathering and organizing information on each client, from basic details to their key challenges and goals.
How to Use the Customer Profile Sheet:

- ✓ Fill in the customer's personal and professional details.
- ✓ Record the customer's current challenges, goals, and how your product or service can help them.
- ✓ Keep notes on any conversations you have with the client, including key takeaways, objections, and potential solutions.

Example:
Let's say you have a new client, a small business

Customer Profile Sheet Template:

Customer Name	Company Name	Contact Info	Challenges	Goals	Notes on Conversations
John Doe	XYZ Corp	[Email/ Phone]	Struggling with lead generation	Increase lead flow by 20%	Interested in digital marketing solutions. Next meeting scheduled for [date]

owner. You would fill out their profile by noting their industry, key business challenges, and the objectives they hope to achieve by using your service.

---

4. Objection Log

Handling objections is a critical skill in sales, and keeping track of common objections helps you improve your responses. The **Objection Log** allows you to document the objections you encounter during the sales process and plan your responses for future interactions.

How to Use the Objection Log:

- ✓ After each interaction, record any objections the customer raised.
- ✓ Note your response to the objection and whether it was effective.
- ✓ Reflect on how you can refine your approach for next time, based on the outcome.

Example:
During a call with a prospect, they mention that your product is too expensive. You would record this objection, how you responded (e.g., by explaining

the long-term value of your solution), and whether it led to a positive outcome.

Objection Log Template:

Date	Customer Name	Objection	Your Response	Outcome	Follow-Up Action
[Date]	Jane Smith	Price is too high	Explained ROI and long-term savings	Customer asked for a demo	Schedule demo for [date]
[Date]	Bob Johnson	Unsure about product compatibility	Offered a technical consultation	Customer requested more info	Send technical specs by [date]

---

5. FAB Worksheet

The FAB (Features, Advantages, Benefits) worksheet helps you translate product features into tangible benefits for your customers. By clearly defining how the features of your product or service will benefit the customer, you can communicate value more effectively during sales presentations.

How to Use the FAB Worksheet:

- ✓ List the key features of your product or service.
- ✓ For each feature, identify the advantage it offers.
- ✓ Translate that advantage into a clear benefit that will resonate with your customer.

Example:

If you sell a software tool, a key feature might be its automation capabilities. The advantage is that it saves time, and the benefit to the customer is that they can focus on growing their business instead of being bogged down by manual tasks.

FAB Worksheet Template:

Feature	Advantage	Benefit (Customer Perspective)
Automated task management	Saves time	Frees up time for strategic business activities
Cloud-based storage	Accessible from anywhere	Increased flexibility and collaboration

---

6. Sales Strategy Template

Having a clear strategy is essential for any successful sales professional. The Sales Strategy Template provides a framework for setting your goals, identifying key actions, and tracking your progress.

How to Use the Sales Strategy Template:

- ✓ Define your sales goals for the upcoming quarter or year.
- ✓ Identify the key actions you will take to reach those goals, such as prospecting efforts, follow-ups, and presentations.
- ✓ Track your progress and adjust your strategy based on results.

Example:

Your goal might be to increase sales by 15% in the next quarter. Your key actions could include increasing outreach to new leads by 20% and scheduling more product demos. You would then track whether these actions are leading to more closed deals and adjust as needed.

Sales Strategy Template:

Sales Goal	Key Actions	Progress Tracking	Adjustments Needed
Increase sales by 15%	Increase outreach to new leads by 20%	Made 50% more calls, scheduled 10 demos	Increase follow-up emails for cold leads

---

7. Customer Follow-Up Template (From Chapter 11)

Maintaining relationships with clients after the sale is critical for customer retention. The Customer Follow-Up Template helps you create a consistent follow-up schedule to stay in touch with your clients.

How to Use the Customer Follow-Up Template:

- ✓ Record each customer interaction, including the type of follow-up (email, phone, meeting), the date of the interaction, and any next steps.
- ✓ Schedule regular follow-ups, such as a thank-you email after the sale, a satisfaction check-in, and an annual review.
- ✓ Use the template to ensure no customer is forgotten and that you maintain regular, meaningful communication.

Example:

After closing a deal with a client, you would use the template to track your follow-up actions—first, a thank-you email, then a call in two weeks to ensure they're happy with the product, and finally, a six-month check-in to offer additional support.

Customer Follow-Up Template:

Date	Customer Name	Interaction Type	Key Points Discussed	Follow-Up Action
[Date]	ABC Company	Phone Call	Product received, no issues so far	Schedule satisfaction call in 1 month
[Date]	XYZ Corporation	Thank-You Email	Expressed thanks for business, next steps	Call to discuss future needs in 3 months

---

These practical worksheets and templates are designed to be used regularly to enhance your productivity, refine your sales approach, and build stronger relationships with your customers. Each tool is crafted to be simple yet powerful, guiding you step by step in key areas such as daily activity management, prospecting, handling objections, and customer follow-ups.

By incorporating these tools into your daily routine, you'll be better equipped to meet your sales goals and deliver exceptional results. Start using these templates today, and remember that consistent action, paired with thoughtful reflection and strategy, will pave the way for long-term success.

Conclusion: Taking Your Sales Journey Forward

Congratulations! You've reached the end of this book, but your journey as a successful salesperson is just beginning. The knowledge, skills, and strategies you've gained are your foundation, but now it's time to take action.

Sales is a profession that requires continuous growth, resilience, and adaptability. Each client interaction is an opportunity to learn, improve, and refine your approach. You have the tools to build meaningful relationships, address challenges head-on, and close deals with confidence. The road ahead may not always be easy, but with every setback comes an opportunity to rise stronger.

Remember, mastery doesn't happen overnight. It's the culmination of daily effort, practice, and reflection. Commit to applying these learnings in your everyday routine, honing your skills with every call, and striving for excellence with every client interaction. Make role-plays and evaluations a part of your system—these are not just exercises but the key to unlocking consistent success.

Be relentless in your pursuit of improvement, but also patient with yourself. Every step forward, no matter how small, is progress. When challenges arise, lean on what you've learned here—your skills in active listening, objection handling, rapport building, and closing will guide you through.

Your journey is unique, and your potential is limitless. You have what it takes to be an extraordinary salesperson. Keep pushing, keep learning, and keep evolving.

I wish you tremendous success as you move forward in your sales career. The world of opportunities is open to those who dare to take the first step and stay committed to their growth. Go out there with confidence, determination, and a mindset to win.

Here's to your success and to the impact you will make in the world of sales. The best is yet to come!

About the Author 'GERARD ASSEY'

Gerard Assey is a Graduate in Economics, a PGD in Management (HRD) and holds a Doctorate in Leadership. Gerard holds several International Qualifications in Sales, Debt Collection, Training & Teaching, and is a 'Fellow' of the prestigious 'Institute of Sales & Marketing Management'-UK, a Certified NLP Practitioner, a 'Certified Trainer', an 'Accredited Management Teacher-Behavioral Sciences', a 'Certified Competency Facilitator', a 'Certified Management Consultant'- (the International credentials of a professional management consultant, awarded in accordance with global standards of the ICMCI); and a Certification from the University of Michigan in 'Successful Negotiation: Essential Strategies and Skills'

He is also a Member of the 'National Association of Sales Professionals' backed with several years experience in varied industries, both in India and Overseas. He also holds an 'Etiquette Consultant' Certification from the USA (by Sue Fox, Author of Best Seller: 'Business Etiquette for Dummies'. She has trained some of the top celebrities' world over). He was also a recipient of a scholarship for extensive training in Japan on 'Corporate Management for India'.

Gerard Assey is 'Founder & Chief Corporate Trainer' of the Group: **'Citius, Altius, Fortius Unlimited'**- an organization that **celebrated 20 years of Glorious Service** in 2021, focusing on 3 Core Competencies:

People. Performance. Profit; in functional areas of Sales & Marketing, HR & Organizational Development, covering Recruitment, Training & Consultancy!

Having managed organizations with large Sales Forces in India & Overseas, his specialization cover extensive areas of Sales Training (All levels - Presentation, Negotiation, Key/ Strategic Accounts Management & Managerial Skills for all sectors), Bid Proposal/ Capture Planning/ Management Trainings, Retail Sales, Customer Service & Customer Retention Programs, Training for Prevention & Collection of Debt, Self & Personal Development Programs (Time Management, Teamwork & Team Building, Business Etiquette & Personal Grooming, Leadership & Managerial Skills, People Management Skills, Train-the-Trainer etc), including preparation of Custom-designed Business Manuals for Internal (HR, Induction, and Sales etc) & External use (Instruction, User Manuals).

Gerard has successfully conducted over 6350 Trainings & Workshops (as of Oct '24) all across India, Middle East, Africa, Europe & S.E. Asia. Besides public programs conducted regularly, both in India & Overseas, he has some of the top names as clients whom he services from Single Owners to large Public & Government undertakings, covering all sectors, for their in-house needs.

His website: www.CollectionSkills.com is the only one in this part of the world to be featured in the 'Collections & Credit Risk Magazine-USA' under 'Who's Who in Training' and ranks TOP, along with other websites listed below on most search engines.

Gerard is author of 154 books already (Oct 2024)

A few of our business related books:

1. Bite-sized Bits on Commonsense Management
2. Heart to Heart on Life's Principles'
3. How to become a Successful Manager
4. The Sales Professionals' Master Workbook of S.Y.S.T.E.M.S
5. The Professional Business Email Etiquette Handbook & Guide
6. The Professional Business Video-Conferencing Etiquette Handbook & Guide
7. Professional Presentation Skills
8. Exceptional Customer Service
9. Professional Tele-Marketing Skills
10. Professional Debt Collection Skills
11. The G.R.E.A.T. Sales & Service Workbook
12. Sales Training Advantage for Results (*The Ultimate Sales Training Manual to enable you stand out as a S.T.A.R.*)
13. CEO Daily Planner & Organizer
14. The Sales Professionals' Master Daily Planner
15. The Professional Debt Collector's Master Daily Planner
16. My Daily Planner & Organizer
17. MY EMERGENCY INFORMATION RECORD (Family Emergency & Peace of Mind Planner)
18. The Ultimate Therapist & Counselors Planner and Organizer
19. Building an Ethical Workplace
20. Managing Relationships at Work
21. Managing Business Meetings Effectively
22. Effective Delegation Skills
23. Goal Setting for Success
24. B2B Selling by Email
25. Professional Business Etiquette & Grooming
26. Dining Etiquette & Table Manners
27. Effective Networking Skills
28. Grooming, Etiquette & Manners for Teens, Young Adults & Future Leaders
29. Inter-Personal Skills
30. Get Ready, Get Hired!
31. Selling in a Recession
32. Effective Receivables Management in an Economic Downturn!
33. Real Estate & Property Sales Training
34. Credit Sales & Accounts Receivable Management
35. Selling Skills for Real Estate & Property Advisors
36. Take G.R.E.A.T. C.A.R.E!
37. Spa, Salon & Health Club Selling Skills
38. Selling Travel, Holiday & MICE Services
39. Selling Skills for Spa's, Salons & Health Clubs
40. Retailing in Salons & Spas
41. Selling Holiday, Vacation, Tours & Packages
42. The Power of Sales Referrals
43. Selling Luxury
44. Technical Selling Skills
45. Financial Advisors Sales Training

46. Dealing with Burnout at Work Monopolize Your Markets
47. Selling to Affluent Customers
48. Growing up with Grace
49. Financial Selling Skills
50. *The Effective Manager's Guide: Key Skills to Thrive*
51. From Aspiring to Inspiring: A Guide for New Managers on the Rise
52. The Power of Focus
53. Selling with Integrity: Sell Like Jesus The Perfect Role Model!
54. 31 Habits of Champions: Your 31-Day Journey to Greatness
55. Rejecting Grasshopper Talk: From Grasshopper to Giant-Killer- *Defeating Giants Daily!*
56. Navigate the AI-Powered Future of Bid & Proposals: Up-Skill to Stay Relevant with Alternative Career Paths & Opportunities
57. Hiring Sales Winners
58. Present with Impact
59. Success Unlocked: *Breaking Free from Habits that Hold You Back*
60. Complaints to Cheers, Feedback to Gold: Mastering Complaints Management
61. Thriving Together: *Cultivating Diversity, Equity, and Inclusion*
62. Coaching Skills for Sales Managers
63. Soaring to Success in Business & Leadership: Swifter, Higher, Stronger!
64. From Classroom to Podium: A Student's Guide to Powerful Public Speaking & Presentation Skills
65. Developing Self-Discipline
66. The CEO's 31-Day Power Plan: Unlocking Success through Essential Traits
67. Credibility Matters
68. A Winning Attitude
69. Bid & Proposal Management Using AI
70. Sales Forecasting: A Practical & Proven Guide to Strategic Sales Forecasting
71. Elevate & Energize: *50 Dynamic & Fun Activities for Peak Workplace Morale*
72. 'Sales SOS! Sales on Fire! *30 Days to Conquer Chaos & the Nightmares of Success!'*
73. Mastering Sales Managerial Skills: *Building High-Performing Teams & Driving Exceptional Results*
74. Eagle-Eyed Leadership: Unleashing the Power of 31 Lessons from Eagles
75. The Ultimate Employee Training Guide: *Training Today, Leading Tomorrow*
76. Being More Accountable at Work
77. Creating a Culture of Continuous Improvement
78. Effective Questioning & Listening Skills

79. The Power of Value Selling
80. The Growth Mindset
81. Mastering Professional Help Desk Skills
82. The Power to Lead with Empathy
83. Being Prepared: The Key to Unlocking Success
84. Youthful Spark-Youth Energizers, Activities and Games-Igniting the Fun in Youth
85. Ignite your Motivation for Success
86. Elevate Your Executive Presence: *Your Roadmap to Executive Excellence*
87. Smart Decisions: *Mastering Problem Solving with Strategic Solutions for Business Success*
88. Strategic Planning: *Developing and Implementing Strategic Plans to Achieve Long-Term Business Goals*
89. The Power of Stay Interviews
90. Developing G.R.I.T.
91. Adaptability
92. Diagnosis- *A Key Skill for Leadership*
93. The Burnout-Proof Salesperson: *The Master Guide to Preventing Stress & Burnout-* Strategies for Thriving in Sales
94. Learning from Failure: *Keys to Success*
95. Customer Success Management
96. Overcoming the Killers of Motivation
97. The C-Suite Code: *Mastering Skills for Executive Excellence'*
98. Dealing with Difficult Customers
99. Unlocking Your Potential: Mastering the Top 20 Life Skills for a Brighter Future
100. Nurturing Tomorrow's Leaders: *Essential Soft Skills Every Child Must Learn*
101. Lively & Fun Party Games for Seniors & Elders
102. Role Playing for Sales Champions: From Practice to Performance
103. Fun and Exciting Party Games for Kids
104. Case Studies for Sales
105. 'Role-Playing for Unbeatable Customer Service
106. Case Studies in Customer Service
107. Case Studies in Winning Negotiations
108. Case Studies in Management & Leadership
109. Case Studies in Human Resources & Talent Management
110. CEO Success Blueprint: The Essential Toolkit for CEOs and C-Level Executives
111. The Salesperson's Self-Coaching Guide: *Master Your Own Self-Coaching Plan for Success*

Besides regularly contributing to business & trade journals, including international ones such as the 'Creative Training Techniques' and the 'Sales News' of the U.S.A, He is also a member of several prestigious bodies & trade associations, having participated in many Conferences & Workshops in India & Overseas.
Prior to his last assignment of leading & managing a large MNC as head, Gerard had a 3-year stint in the Middle East as a Consultant with a leading British Consultancy Firm.

As the past 'Official Country Representative' for the International Business Award- 'THE STEVIES'-(the business world's own Oscar) for about 4 years- he ensured a few Indian companies that qualify for the same every year!

Gerard can be contacted at:
Email: training@Sales-Training.in,training@CollectionSkills.com
Websites:

www.Sales-Training.in
www.EtiquetteWorks.in
www.CollectionSkills.com
www.RetailSalesTraining.in
www.SalesTrainingIndia.com
www.ManualPreparation.com
www.TrainingWithPuppets.com
www.FirstContactAcademy.com
www.SalesAndMarketingRecruiter.com

Our TRAININGS that can help your team

- ✓ **Sales Effectiveness**: Selling Skills for any Sector: Service/ Logistics/ FMCG Realty/ Insurance & Finance/ Media/ SPA's, Health Clubs & Salons/ Key Account Management, Effective Negotiation Skills/ Bid & Proposal Management Skills/ Retail Sales Training: Any Sector (Auto, Jewelry, Clothing, Luxury etc)
- ✓ **Customer Service Skills**-Complaints Handling & Customer Retention
- ✓ **Debt Prevention & Collection Skills**
- ✓ **Etiquette & Grooming**
- ✓ **Leadership & Managerial Skills**
- ✓ **Self & Personal Development Skills**: Presentation Skills/ Effective Communication Skills/Business Proposal Writing Skills/ Problem Solving & Decision Making Skills/ Empowering Secretaries-The perfect PA! (For Secretaries & PA's)/ Effective Time Management/ Teamwork & Teambuilding/ P.R.I.D.E- **P**ersonal **R**esponsibility **I**n **D**elivering **E**xcellence

www.ingramcontent.com/pod-product-compliance
Ingram Content Group UK Ltd.
Pitfield, Milton Keynes, MK11 3LW, UK
UKHW021340190726
13845UKWH00027B/644

9 788197 965487